MIND
over
MUFFIN
TOP

Gina
Thank you so much!
for coming to the party!
I hope you enjoy the book &
that it inspires you to be your
best self!
Cheryl Keaney

Cheryl Keaney

26 25 24 23 22 21   8 7 6 5 4 3 2 1

MIND OVER MUFFIN TOP
Copyright ©2021 Cheryl Keaney

Published by:
Emerge Publishing, LLC
9521 B Riverside parkway, Suite 243
Tulsa, OK 74137
Phone: 888.407.4447
www.emerge.pub

Library of Congress Cataloging-in-Publication Data:
ISBN: 978-1954966-09-3 Perfect Bound

Printed in the United States

TABLE OF CONTENTS

DEDICATION

To my father, for teaching me that I miss 100% of the shots I don't take.
I love you dad!

ACKNOWLEDGMENTS

Antonella Avena, for always believing in me, and for your continued love and support. Thanks for your helpful feedback and thoughts during the writing of this book.

To Catherine, for your help with editing and ideas. I'm so glad to have you for a neighbor and friend.

To Bobbi, for your insight and help in the writing of this book. Thanks for being such a great friend.

Meghann Perry, my recovery coach, for your amazing strength, wisdom and guidance. I cannot thank you enough. I could not have done this without you.

Jessica Verwys, for your friendship, love and support. Thanks for always being there for me — you're like the sister I never had.

To the wonderful team at Emerge Publishing, for helping to fulfill a life dream in writing this book.

And to my amazing family and friends, I love and appreciate all of you.

ENDORSEMENTS

"In this book, Cheryl weaves her lifelong dedication to holistic health together with over 30 years of professional experience and education, and presents readers with a comprehensive guide for transforming their health and wellness. A knowledgeable and compassionate guide, Cheryl motivates and assists readers in finding lasting solutions for building a healthier life." -- *Kate Bommarito, certified health coach, owner of BommLiving: Living the Life You Love*

"Cheryl is an exceptional soul. Her ability to relate to people from all walks of life has allowed her to share her vast knowledge of health and fitness. She enables them to take back control, to live a happier and healthier life. It is refreshing to see her create such a compilation — with insight, structure and sweeping scope that centers on the health of the entire individual." -- *Pattie A., former client*

"If you struggle with consistency when it comes to sticking to a diet or fitness plan, this book is for you! Cheryl makes this book relatable and easy to understand. Her passion to help others succeed has led her to be regarded as one of the best personal trainer and nutrition coaches around. She guides you through a journey to living a healthier lifestyle, and being stronger in body and mind." -- *Traci Hofmann, CPT, SimpliFit4U owner*

"Cheryl's passion for health and her desire to help individuals achieve their fitness goals are inspiring. This book is the tool you need to begin and maintain a journey to a healthier you." -- *Bobbi Alton, inspired client*

"*Mind Over Muffin Top* is brilliant simplicity at its best. I love how Cheryl doesn't overcomplicate it. Her connection and examples are very inspiring and easy to comprehend for all populations. This book comes from an individual who seeks answers and produces results. She's a caring, passionate woman in the health and fitness industry who serves with love. I love her foundation and mindset analogy. Nicely done!!!" -- *Brandi Leverenz, DC*

"Take care of your body. It's the only place you have to live."
—*Jim Rohn*

INTRODUCTION

In today's society, we are bombarded with an overload of information when it comes to diet and exercise. There is so much conflicting advice on what's the best way to lose weight, the best supplement to take for this or that, the best exercise, etc. And with the thousands of books, apps, videos, etc. on diet and exercise, people are clueless as to where to start or what to do. It's overwhelming, and it doesn't have to be.

What I've come to realize over the course of my 22-plus years in the fitness industry, is that it's not about finding the perfect diet, exercise plan or supplement to take. It's not that complicated, and actually quite simple.

Success starts with building a solid foundation!

What do I mean by this?

Think of our bodies as the house we live in. Jim Rohn's quote above hits the nail on the head, and it's what made me think of seeing our bodies as a house.

Our "house" is simply four key parts — a foundation, two pillars and a roof. Diet is one pillar, exercise the second pillar and our mindset the roof.

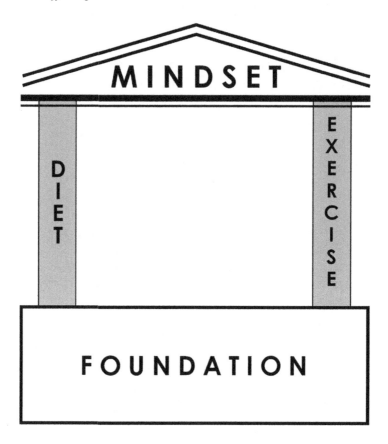

The foundation supports the pillars, the pillars support the roof and the roof protects the underlying pillars and foundation. Each part is vitally important and functions best in correlation with the other parts, supporting and complementing each other versus operating solely on their own.

Like when someone builds a house, the foundation gets built first — before any pillars, walls, roof, etc. When it comes to our health and fitness goals, we too need to start by laying the groundwork for success by building that solid foundation first and foremost.

What does that foundation consist of?

The ability to manage stress, get adequate sleep, have a positive home environment, make yourself a priority, self-care, life balance, time management, goals and healthy habits.

All components of the foundation are vitally important, as they interrelate and affect one another.

AND the key parts of our house are all equally important, as the foundation, pillars and roof all interrelate as well.

If one key part of your "house" weakens, it can affect and weaken the others. If one is optimized and strengthened, it will help support and strengthen the others.

The Pillars — Diet and Exercise

The pillars that are essential to our bodies, aka the "house" we live in, are diet and exercise. The Diet Pillar equates to one's nutrition plan, everything one would eat or drink in a typical day. The Exercise Pillar equates to the amount of activity someone gets and the exercise plan they're doing (if any).

Your diet and exercise habits greatly affect your body. What you eat, when you eat it, if you exercise, or don't exercise — it all matters and it all interrelates.

The pillars of diet and exercise each interrelate with each other, and each is a vital part.

Just like the pillars of a house become weak and can collapse with a weak foundation, so can the pillars (diet and exercise plan) of our body's "house." If the foundation falters, the pillars will eventually falter. If the pillars aren't strong and stable enough, they will crumble. AND just like a house, trying to get by with just one pillar isn't going to work either.

If you want to lose weight through only diet or through only exercise, you will not be able to achieve optimal health and fitness levels and will continue to struggle with achieving your goals.

I see way too many wobbly pillars (poor diet and exercise plans), weak foundations and leaky roofs (negative mindset). No wonder people's health and fitness goals come tumbling down. Many will find themselves falling off track, and being derailed once again.

AND most people don't know that you can lose more than twice as much body fat when you combine exercise and diet, versus just only dieting, or only exercising to lose weight.

As great as exercise is for you, it won't be effective unless you have a balanced nutrition plan supporting your weight loss efforts.

You can't out-exercise a bad diet. And if you only diet, you can lose weight but you can wreak havoc on your metabolism and set yourself up for future weight gain. We'll have none of that, as you are going to learn how to strengthen your pillars by optimizing your diet and exercise plan.

The Roof — Mindset

Our mindset plays a critical role in coping with life and the ability to achieve success. One's mindset is just like the roof of a house. In good shape, it protects the interior of a home from the elements. In poor shape, it can leak and lead to damage of the internal structures (including the pillars and foundation).

In order for our bodies (aka the house we live in) to be protected, we need a strong and protective mindset.

A positive mindset is a like having a strong and sturdy roof.

It will protect us from the harsh elements of life — like stress and the struggles of life. On the other hand, a negative mindset is like having a leaky roof. Over time, the leaks will erode away and can cause damage to our pillars (diet and exercise plan) and our foundation.

Why do people fail at achieving their goals? And why do people fall off the wagon, time after time, and struggle to get back on track?

1. They fail to develop and strengthen the solid foundation that is crucial in one's ability to achieve their goals.

2. They just try to diet or exercise, without really knowing key foundational knowledge to optimize their results.

3. They fail to maintain a positive mindset.

The absolute key to success is having a "house" that is FIT and STRONG in all four key parts — the foundation, diet pillar, exercise pillar, and roof (mindset).

My goals for this book are to:

— help you develop a solid and strong foundation that is the core of any successful fitness plan — by maximizing the strength of each foundational component.

— optimize the strength and longevity of the other key elements of your "house": your pillars (diet and exercise) and (mindset).

— teach you key principles about diet, exercise and the power of a positive mindset.

Mind over muffin top is so much more than just losing that extra weight we carry around our mid-section, it's about developing a mindset that allows you to finally achieve your goals and become your best self.

Learn why calorie counting isn't enough, how to deal with diet saboteurs, how to increase your body's ability to burn fat, and create a positive mindset to believe and achieve!

Learn how to empower your mind and overcome the struggles you face. Learn how to accomplish your fitness goals, finally get the results you've so longed for and be inspired to become healthier. It all starts in your mind, and with your mind you can overcome and achieve.

Like a train that goes too fast can derail, you can't rush things when it comes to making the changes needed to achieve your goals, nor do you need to. This book will help you lay down the track you need to achieve your health and fitness goals one step at a time. By taking the time to read this book and do the activities (highly suggested), you will gain the knowledge, hope and motivation needed to fuel the way to everlasting success!

1

THE FOUNDATION

*"You can't build a great building on a weak foundation.
You must have a solid foundation if you're going to have a
strong superstructure."* Gordan B. Hinkley

CREATING A FANTABULOUS FOUNDATION

"Fantabulous," I think it's my new favorite word. By definition, it's slang for something that is remarkably good. Then you have the word "foundation," which when used as a construction term, serves to keep a building standing strong — especially amidst the forces of nature that can wreak havoc. When it comes to building a foundation, it is something that you need to do remarkably well. Of course, the more remarkable the better. And like the quote above, if you want your "house" to be the superstructure that it has the potential to be, you need to build a solid foundation.

In the following chapters you will learn about the following key components needed to do just that:

Stress – how to manage and reduce its negative effects

Sleep – why it's vital for health, energy and motivation

Home Environment – why it's important to minimize clutter, be organized, and how feng shui can help improve health and success

Prioritize Self – why saying yes to yourself and taking care of your needs first is important in accomplishing your goals

Self-care – how implementing self-care improves your mental health and well-being

Life Balance – why it's key for overall happiness and health

Time Management – how to prioritize and plan, and find much-needed time

Goals – why it is important to start with small steps, create healthy habits, and how to develop the motivation to achieve them

Habits - ability to develop and sustain healthy habits

"The future depends on what you do today."
—*Mahatma Gandhi*

YOUR FUTURE SELF

Have you ever looked in the mirror and imagined seeing yourself 10, 20 or 30-plus years from now? Think of how you are going to feel looking in the mirror years from now. When thinking forward and imagining your future self, you want to not only be grateful, but proud of your past choices. That reflection of yourself will truly be a reflection of you, the choices you have made and the life experiences you have accumulated.

You definitely do not want your future reaction to be, "Oh my gosh, I wish I took better care of myself."

Our future depends on the choices we make today, and it starts by putting our minds to it. I think there is no better way to start off on this journey to developing a solid foundation without first keeping this in mind. Doing so will not only help inspire you, but motivate you to take the action and steps needed to achieve ultimate success.

What do you want to see when you look in that mirror and see your future self?

Are you making choices in your life that your future self will be happy for?

Like the sand in an hourglass, we only have so much time and our sand is trickling down bit by bit.

How you live your life will not only determine how fast you use up your sand, but how you feel on a daily basis. For the most part, we are all given an equal amount of sand at birth. What is happening is that a lot of people are not taking care of themselves and have unhealthy habits. In essence, their sand is emptying much quicker. Years of their life are being lost, and they are accelerating the aging of their bodies and minds.

BUT with a healthy lifestyle, you can increase your longevity, and, in a sense, add sand to your hourglass.

If you take care of yourself, you will be much happier with what you see than if you do not.

You can choose to exercise, cut back on sugar, quit smoking, drink less alcohol and make sleep a priority. You can choose not to as well, but remember, that you are choosing who is going to be looking back at you years from now.

Think about this — a stressed individual probably does not sleep much. Because of that, they tend to drink an excess of coffee (which dehydrates you). They do not sleep due to stress and/or the excess of the caffeine, so therefore they are too tired and lack the motivation to exercise. In addition, because of the stress and lack of sleep, they will typically crave and overindulge in comfort foods that are high in fat and sugar. They are lacking sleep, not eating healthy and not exercising. It is very well possible that he/she could also be overindulging in alcohol and smoking cigarettes in attempts to deal with the stress. Everything in this chain of events is very toxic to the body and accelerates aging.

This type of behavior leads to an hourglass that is losing sand pretty darn quick, and any resemblance to an hourglass figure probably is not looking so hot on top of that. That will lead to additional health problems as well. What does your hourglass look like? Do all you can to help yourself live a longer, happier and healthy life and keep that hourglass sand trickling down as slow as you can.

We cannot go back and change what we have done in the past, but we can start making choices today our future selves will be thankful for. Remember what got you here. The choices of your past brought you to where you are now.

You can start making choices today to get you to where you want to go, and to being the person you want to be.

One step at a time and one choice at a time — you can create the you that you desire to be!

Mackie's Story

Mackie is a force to be reckoned with. A former collegiate athlete, she excelled in multiple sports: basketball, softball, field hockey and tennis. After college, she went on to teach aerobic classes and continued playing some sports recreationally. She got married, had two kids and still managed to fit exercise in her busy schedule — all while keeping a balance in her life.

When her youngest son was three years old, she set her mind to accomplish a lifetime goal of hers: to run a marathon. "It was a big goal for me, something I always wanted to accomplish." Mackie would run in the mornings before work, and then do track workouts after work, getting a 10-year-old babysitter to watch her son while she did her sprint work on the track. And guess who that 10-year-old babysitter was? Me! I remember watching her son, Ben, riding his big wheel on the outskirts of the track, while Mackie raced by, lap after lap. Her dedication was remarkable, even to a young kid like me.

Mackie not only accomplished running her first ever marathon, but running in and finishing 12 more. "If I start, I'm finishing. Not everyone that starts, finishes."

Years later, she had to get a knee replacement and had to stop running. BUT of course, that didn't stop her. She resiliently switched her passion to biking: "I never let anything slow me down. I always found a way to stay active." At 73 years of age, she bikes/trikes over 4000 miles a year, and walks several times a week.

"I never had an acute illness. I just always exercised to feel better. I need to be out there, for mental and physical health." Mackie also realizes the importance of keeping her brain healthy, and does a variety of things to exercise that as well. "I do crossword puzzles, word jumbles, cross-stitch, crochet and read. Keeping our brain healthy, as you know, is just as important."

Mackie's active lifestyle has kept her young in body, mind and spirit — she not only adds sand to her hourglass, but enjoys and experiences a higher quality of life because of it. She has always has been, and continues to be, a huge inspiration to me.

Mind Over Muffin Top Activity

Imagine the person you want to see looking back at yourself a year from now, two years from now, and so on.

What kind of choices is that new you making?

What choices can you start making today?

"It's not stress that kills us it is our reaction to it."
—Hans Selye

GET A GRIP

Stress takes a toll on all of us. It literally takes years off our lives and accelerates the aging process. Known as the "silent killer," it can rob your muscle, sleep and health. Its effects are very harmful to the human body.

Have you ever compared pictures of past presidents before and after they took office? The often look far more than several years older by the time they leave office. Sometimes the effects of stress are visible, but the unseen effects can be the real killer.

It's often the major culprit in a long list of serious health problems — diabetes, asthma, obesity, high blood pressure, heart disease and depression. It's been estimated that 80–90% of all disease is caused by stress.

77% of people regularly experience physical symptoms of stress, and 73% of people experience psychological symptoms. The negative physical, mental and emotional effects on your body are nothing to take lightly. The symptoms can be numerous: anxiety and depression, loss of appetite, insomnia, migraines, high or low blood pressure, and gastrointestinal and heart problems. Stress also takes a toll on our immune system by increasing the odds of getting sick and prolonging recovery rate if you are sick.

When it comes to our health and fitness goals, excessive stress and the inability to handle it effectively can have detrimental effects on us. Stress affects your ability to sleep and the quality of your sleep, which is vital for your health and well-being.

The ability to manage stress is a crucial component of a solid foundation.

Stress also increases the hormones cortisol and insulin, which cause an increase in appetite and weight gain, especially around our waistline. It also breaks down muscle, lowers metabolism and weakens your immune system. Have you ever noticed an increased desire for comfort foods when under a lot of stress? Our desire to eat these tasty, high-fat and high-sugar foods are often because of that.

In addition, lack of sleep causes stress on your body, and with it, an increase in cortisol levels. Lack of sleep also causes our body's leptin cells (produced by your fat cells) to decrease, and ghrelin (produced by your stomach) to increase. This creates an energy deficiency and appetite confusion. You get the double whammy of this stress and poor sleep combo. AND what would the likely result of someone stressed, tired, hungry and craving sweets be? Eating donuts, junk food and generally not giving a (blank) about what you eat. You're too tired and too hungry to care. Then, if you eat those high-fat and sugar foods, you end up zapping your energy levels even more so.

I know when I'm lacking sleep, I don't want to grocery shop, cook, clean, let alone exercise. It's no wonder when one is dealing with more stress in their life, their motivation goes right down the tubes. Lack of sleep leads to a lack of energy, which leads to a lack of motivation.

When our bodies and minds are stressed, it's even more important to get adequate rest to rejuvenate and replenish our energy stores and immune system.

What is the best way to reduce stress and sleep better? In my opinion, nothing beats exercise. I find it to be the most important and beneficial thing there is.

BUT how are you going to have the motivation to do much of anything, let alone exercise, when you're feeling depressed and exhausted from lack of sleep?

What does motivation start with? Other than the letter "M," like my father would say, "it starts with sleep." How are you going to feel like working out or have the energy to work out on four hours of sleep? If you need to go grocery shopping, think that will happen? Think you'll have the energy to cook a healthy meal? Likely not.

Do you see the connection? You need to exercise first, to give your body an outlet for the stress, so that you can relax at night and get a good night's sleep.

Exercise is the best thing you can do to relieve stress and anxiety.

Multiple research studies have shown that exercise helps decrease insomnia, improve the quality of sleep and that it can have effects similar to a sleeping pill. And conversely, insomnia is associated with a lack of exercise. Those that have a regular exercise routine tend to have less sleep issues or suffer from insomnia.

People often say they're too tired to work out, maybe from lack of sleep (caused by stress) or being too drained physically and mentally (caused by stress). It becomes more important than ever to exercise to reduce and relieve stress, which in turn will help you to sleep better. They all interrelate and have an effect on the other.

Just going for a simple, leisurely walk after dinner can help relieve stress and help you to sleep better.

It's important to just do something, as any form of exercise is beneficial in combating the negative effects of stress. Whether you go for a walk, jog, lift weights, or play *Wii Fit*, they're all beneficial in helping to relieve stress. A little exercise can go a long way in helping to decrease the negative impact stress causes.

We need to get a grip on stress, and not let it take a grip on us. Beat this "silent killer" to have a happier and healthier day today and in the days to come.

Mind Over Muffin Top Tip

Limit watching the news to 2–3 hours a day, and be sure to palette cleanse afterwards by doing something enjoyable (laugh, sing, dance) and/or engaging enough to crowd out the negative thoughts and images.

"You cannot buy your health; you must earn it through healthy living."
—Joel Fuhrman

GETTING YOUR ZZZS

Getting adequate sleep is like gold, and it should be valued and treated as the treasure it really is. To be wealthy in health, we need the gold that is sleep. Sleep is crucial to our health, energy and motivation, and it's a vital component to one's foundation.

Just like cracks in the foundation of a house can cause it to crumble, sleep can cause cracks in the foundation of your health and fitness goals. When the foundation gives, the pillars (diet and exercise plan) start to weaken. If not fixed, the cracks will worsen and eventually cause a total collapse — your goals, diet and exercise plan (the pillars) will collapse right along with it.

The results from a 2018 study, involving 10,000 people, showed that lack of sleep affects our body's ability to function. The people that fell below the 7–8-hour sleep range, demonstrated that the lack of sufficient sleep had a negative effect on their verbal and reasoning skills, planning and decision making. I know I sure notice that at work and in writing this book. I can't focus, think clearly and have little motivation to do much of anything.

Several other studies have shown that if you sleep better, you age better. This is because your body produces human growth hormone during sleep, which has potent fat-burning and muscle-building capabilities. It's a huge benefit to sleep that most people aren't aware of. You definitely don't want to miss out on that!

Lack of sleep and decreased human growth hormone can lead to weight gain, loss of muscle mass, decreased immune function, decreased memory function and insulin resistance (diabetes). Not getting adequate sleep also is known to put your health at risk — it can also increase risk of stroke, heart disease and overall chances of having an early death.

When it comes to one's health and fitness goals, getting adequate sleep is vital for maximizing your fat loss and muscle building efforts.

It's also greatly important for simply having the energy and motivation to be active and of a healthy mindset. In order to sleep though, we need to be able to wind down. The goal in winding down is to reduce stress, relax and have the calm that is needed for good quality sleep.

It is advised not to watch television or use your phone/computer two hours prior to going to bed, as the blue light stimulates our brains and delays our bodies internal clock. This can cause our body's sleep-inducing hormone, melatonin, to be suppressed and make it more difficult to fall asleep.

Also, be sure to avoid drinking alcohol as it greatly decreases the quality of sleep.

Try to go to bed and get up at the same time every morning to help your body get in a sleep routine. If your sleep schedule is all over the place, it will make it that much harder for you to get sleep at night and wake up in the morning. We plug our phones in to charge at night, but we aren't fully charging our own batteries.

Having a regular sleep schedule and getting the recommended 7–8 hours of sleep a night is an important habit that shouldn't be overlooked.

Having a hard time sleeping? If you don't already have one, a weighted blanket might be just what you need. These blankets help with lessening anxiety to help you relax and fall asleep. I bought one myself last year, and it's done wonders. If I find myself tossing and turning, I grab my weighted blanket and let it do its magic. As soon as it covers me, I instantly feel a sense of calm. It's amazing how comforting it is and how much it helps.

Another thing that could cause difficulty sleeping is a room that is too bright. I noticed that in my bedroom there was a lot of light coming in from my neighbor's porch light and the light poles in the parking lot. I finally put up some blackout curtains and started noticing how much faster I was falling asleep. What a difference! An added bonus to the blackout curtains, is that they help with cancelling out outdoor noise. The extra sense of calm and quiet I now feel has helped tremendously in improving the overall quality of my sleep.

Many people are unaware of how much light directly affects our ability to fall asleep. Even the light from your cell phone or electronic devices in your bedroom can affect you. Try to minimize any source of light in your room to maximize your ability to fall asleep and stay asleep.

A good night's sleep is one of the most important things you can do for yourself. Sleep brings with it more energy, motivation, health and happiness. Start getting some Zzzs and reap the wealth of health benefits it provides. Start putting some sand back in your hourglass!

Mind Over Muffin Top Activity

What does your sleep schedule look like?

Do you need to get more sleep?

If so, what can you do to get more sleep?

What can you do to improve the quality of your sleep?

"Clutter is not just the stuff on your floor — it's anything that stands between you and the life you want to be living."
—Peter Walsh

DISCOVER AND DECLUTTER

Our homes and living space have a huge impact on our energy and stress levels, much more than most people realize. Clutter can increase levels of anxiety, stress and depression, as well as affect our ability to sleep and focus.

Studies have shown that our physical environments can dramatically influence our emotions, behaviors and cognitive ability. One study even found that cortisol levels increased in the mothers whose homes were cluttered.

Even sleeping in a cluttered room will likely increase the chances one will suffer from sleep problems.

If that isn't enough, there are multiple studies showing a link between clutter and unhealthy eating choices. Participants subjected to clutter were found to eat more snacks and twice as many cookies than the participants that were in an organized kitchen environment. Did you know that someone is twice as likely to eat a chocolate bar versus an apple in a messy room?

The more cluttered one's home is, the more likely they are to have a weight problem.

According to studies, an alarming 77% of people inhighly-cluttered homes will become overweight. On the flip side, people that had cleaner and more organized homes were proven to be more active and in better physical health.

Our lives need decluttering, both physically and digitally. Our brains have a limited number of functions they can perform at one time, and clutter and distractions take up mental energy and brain space.

The things that really aren't worth our attention take up space that is needed for our overall thinking process and other matters of importance.

AND what matters most is creating an environment that supports your health and well-being. Discover what decluttering can do for you. In freeing up your space, you free up your mind to allow yourself to focus on what matters to you most.

I remember being quite surprised after coming home from work one dayand finding a clean kitchen with no dishes in the sink, especially since there was quite a *Jenga*-like mountain of dishes in the sink when I left. Other than the pleasant surprise of not having to do the dishes, I realized how happy and energetic I felt walking in to a clean kitchen. Not only that, but my mind felt clearer, and I finally accomplished a lot of work tasks that needed to get done that evening.

It made me realize how many things could be draining people's energy, and therefore affecting their ability to achieve their goals. It was eye opening to me, and quite interesting as well. I thought to myself, this is partly what feng fhui is about: coming home to a calm and relaxing environment. I told myself that I needed to get back to doing more of it, as well as encourage others to do the same.

Mind Over Muffin Top Activity

What clutter do you experience in your life? In your home?

What can you do to decrease the clutter?

What can you do in your home to be more organized?

"When home feels out of control, no matter what the reason, unsettledness and anxiety can seep in, and then the chaos internal as well as external."
—*Myquillyn Smith*

FENG SHUI FIT

Ever notice the difference in how you feel when you walk into a clean and organized room versus one that looks like a tornado hit it? If you had a long, hard day at work and you come home to a messy house, it will drain your energy even more.

Ignoring the dirty dishes piled up in the sink, dealing with a constant barrage of text message dings on your phone or living in a cluttered home — all energy drainers. When we ignore something it takes energy, then the brain becomes overwhelmed and we lose the ability to control our thoughts and focus.

Let's say that you had plans to go to the gym that evening. That messy house might just zap the last of your energy reserves, leaving you stressed out, eating cookies on the couch and watching television instead of going to the gym.

See my point?

So, what do you do about this? You feng shui!

What in the heck is feng shui, and how can it relate to health and fitness?

To put it simply, feng shui is an ancient Chinese art and science for improving one's environment — creating a balance and flow of good energy for increased success, health and wellness.

There are several methods, techniques and philosophies. Some involve the use of color and furniture placement. For example, people typically paint bedrooms in soft, relaxing colors. That's along the lines of what feng shui is about: helping you to benefit the most from your environment.

Being organized and clutter free helps save time and energy, what people often state they are lacking. The first book I ever read about feng shui was about clearing your clutter. The book claimed that by clearing the clutter in your life, you could increase your energy and improve your health. It seemed interesting, so I thought, "Hey, it can't hurt; it's worth giving it a try."

I cleaned out my closet, organized my things, moved furniture around and put it to the test. Guess what? It worked. I started to notice how much better I felt when I was at home. I had more energy and didn't feel as drained as I typically would. More energy meant more energy to workout, more energy to get to the grocery store and more energy to cook healthy food.

Being able to come home and feel relaxed meant I wasn't stressed, which equated to improved health and better sleep. I slept better; I felt better. It's time to get your feng shui fit on! It did wonders for me, and it could do some pretty amazing things for you as well.

Mind Over Muffin Top Activity

What can you do in your home to be more organized?

What can you do to create a more relaxing environment in your home?

"Love yourself first, and everything else falls in line. You really
have to love yourself to get anything done in this world."
—Lucille Ball

PUTTING YOURSELF FIRST

How often are you putting yourself first in your life? So many things in our life demand our time and energy, leaving us with little or no time to do things that are important for our health and well-being. Whether it's work, kids, family or friends, we often put other people's needs before our own. Whether it's working more than you should, or skimping out on sleep and exercise, it's easy to put yourself (and your fitness goals) on the back burner and let other things or people take precedence.

You need to take time for yourself and take care of yourself first.

If you're always doing for others and not doing for yourself, you will end up paying the price. What does this lead to? Poor health, a lack of energy and increased stress on the body and mind — all leading to an increased risk of illness and disease.

The key is balance, to give back *and* do for yourself — as much, if not more than you do for others.

As good as it is to do things that benefit or help others, we should not be doing them if they compromise our health, happiness or well-being. If you aren't healthy, not only do you suffer, but everyone you care for then suffers as well. Get the picture?

Putting yourself first means that you realize that you can't help others if you don't care for yourself first.

It doesn't mean that you don't care or that you are a bad person — you just can't give from an empty cup. Imagine carrying a water bottle with you every day. You need to drink from it to stay hydrated and get you through your day. If you give all your water away, you end up dehydrated and fatigued, and have nothing left to give. You are the one that suffers.

Putting yourself first is not selfish, but a necessity.

Here are some tips on how to achieve that:

Sleep

Taking care of yourself starts with sleep, as you learned in a previous chapter.

Without adequate sleep, you won't have much energy or motivation to do much of anything. Lack of sleep increases stress on your body and mind, and compromises your immune system. Sleep is crucial, for it is one of the easiest and best ways to preserve and restore your body, and keep it healthy.

Learn to Say No

Time is precious and it needs to be valued. You have the power of how you spend your time and who you spend it with. This is where learning to say "no" to people is of huge importance. One can only juggle so many things at once. You have to say "yes" to yourself first, and only say "yes" to others if it's something you truly want to do. You also have to think about if you really have the time and energy for it too.

Do what feeds your soul, your heart and what is truly worthy to you.

Saying no to others is saying yes to yourself. Think of times when others said no to you. Did you understand? I totally understand when I'm said no to. I admire that ability in people, for I see that they take care of their needs and put themselves first. You have a choice — don't always feel like you have to be a people-pleaser and say yes to everyone.

Think about if you were told you only had six months to live. I imagine knowing that would truly increase the value you place on your time. Do what makes you happiest and what is healthiest for you, both mentally and physically.

Make Time for Yourself

Make time for yourself and stick to it. Make sure to get regular exercise and schedule times to unwind and relax as well — whether it's a night out with friends, a massage or yoga class. You need time to yourself to de-stress and re-energize yourself so you can stay healthy and productive.

It's time to start putting yourself first — no one can take better care of you than you can!

Mind Over Muffin Top Activity

What are examples of ways that you are not putting yourself first?

What toll is this having on you?

How can you start putting yourself first?

"Taking good care of you, means the people in your life will receive the best of you, rather than what's left of you."
—Carl Bryan.

SIGNIFICANCE OF SELF-CARE

Most of us have all heard how important it is to take care of yourself, but how often are we actually doing it? We know it's important, but do we really know how important it is or how to really do it? Practice self-care and manage stress before it manages and damages you. It is a critical need for one's mental and physical well-being.

So how do you go about implementing self-care? First, it involves listening to your body and your inner self. Do a selfcheck-in, and give yourself breaks when needed and do whatever it is that will allow you to laugh, smile, relax and enjoy yourself. It is crucial for both physical and mental health.

Even several short sixty-second breaks during the day are better than staying in a constant state of tension and stress.

Without it, you risk burnout and the ability to function at work or take care of others. We need the mental vacation, and we need to try and negate the effects of stress on our bodies.

The key is to just do it, do something to take care of you, and make self-care a priority.

If you are not currently practicing self-care, I hope you will now be inspired to start. With the ability to unwind and relax, we gain the calm necessary for sleep. Then, when we sleep better, we create more time, energy and motivation. It is a crucial component to not only help you get through your day better, but to be happier and healthier overall.

RELAX TO THE MAX

No time to relax? It's about time you start trying to change that, and maximize on the benefits it can provide you. When you feel like you don't have time to relax is when you actually need it the most. When you're under constant stress, it wears and tears you down, mentally and physically. One must counter its negative effects, and meditation, deep breathing, massage and yoga are all exceptional ways to do so. A Harvard Medical School study showed that long-term practitioners of relaxation methods, such as yoga and meditation, had far more active "disease-fighting genes" compared to those who practiced no form of relaxation.

The changes were from what they call "the relaxation effect," a phenomenon that could be just as powerful as any medical drug, but without the side effects. In just two months, the genes that fight inflammation, kill diseased cells, and protect the body from cancer, all began to become active. It is so important in our busy, hectic and stressful lives to find the time to unwind. If we don't unwind, we will eventually wind up sick from it.

Personally, I love yoga (which often incorporates meditation). The huge stress relief and relaxation effect I feel afterwards is amazing. As much as I love my yoga class, beforehand I typically feel too stressed and overwhelmed to do it. I then think that I don't have the time or the ability to be still that long and do nothing.

BUT I tell myself that is exactly why I need it — that I need to be still, and that my mind and body need to relax in order to benefit from it. At the beginning of class my mind races as always, but by the middle of class I am lying on my mat with my eyes closed, so relaxed that I feel like I could fall asleep. I am always amazed at the relaxation effect and how much better I feel afterwards. It reinforces why I desperately need it and why I cannot afford not to do it. I cannot afford or continue to let the stress increase my blood pressure, weaken my immune system, drain my energy and deprive my sleep.

Meditation is also a great way to relax your mind and body. It is something you can do anywhere, even closing the office door for a few minutes will do wonders. It allows your brain to enter a state of functioning similar to sleep and helps one to build their resilience to stress. I practice that at home sometimes as well and find it greatly beneficial.

It does not necessarily have to be yoga or mediation (which I highly recommend though). It can be anything that works for you. As long as it quiets your mind and body, that's all that matters. Even something as simple as lighting some candles and playing some soft music at home can help transform the energy of your home to one that's more relaxing and peaceful.

My absolute favorite do-nothing-at-all self-care therapy is getting a massage. My worries and stress disappear, my body and mind relax and my muscle tightness and tension are erased. AND there are numerous health benefits to boot.

Yoga, meditation and massage are wonderful ways to practice self-care, but they may not be for everyone. There are many other wonderful ways to practice self-care and relieve stress — like reading, artwork, crafts, exercise, listening to music, fishing, golfing and playing games. If you are able to do anything outdoors, get out there, for it typically helps one to relax more and get one's mind off things. Whatever it is that works for you, do it. The relaxation aspect is needed for your health and preventing chronic stress from the toll it takes on your body.

Mind Over Muffin Top Tip

Take a bath at night to help reduce the stress and anxiety from the day.

"Self-care means giving yourself permission to pause."
—*Cecilia Tran*

THE MAGIC OF MASSAGE

If there was a way to improve your health and relieve stress without diet or exercise, would you do it? No, I'm not selling a magical pill, but in fact it's quite like a magical pill because it requires no effort at all on your part. It's the magic of massage, in that it's a healing tool in and of itself, with proven health benefits. Numerous studies have shown that massage is not just a luxurious spa treatment anymore. There are actual physiological and psychological changes that occur which have shown to improve overall health and well-being. Let us count the ways!

Stress Reduction

80–90% of disease is stress related, so it's extremely important to keep stress levels to a minimum. In my opinion, nothing is more relaxing than getting a massage. Stress elevates cortisol levels in your body, and studies have shown that cortisol levels are significantly lower after a massage. Our lives can be a constant barrage of stress, and the damage from cortisol wreaks havoc on our health.

Blood Pressure

A 2005 study at the University of South Florida showed that massage helped to significantly improve blood pressure readings in a group of hypertension patients. One group simply received just 10 minutes of massage, 10 times a week, over a three-week period, compared to a control group that just rested. I would much rather treat myself to a regular massage vs. having to get on costly meds.

Sleep

Our minds and bodies don't function well without it. Getting the recommended 7–8 hours of sleep a night is crucial for optimal health and immune function. Not only that, but you need sleep in order to be able to focus and have the energy and motivation to get through your day. Think about how you feel after a night without sleep — not good. A few nights without sleep and you're likely to get run down and end up being sick on top of it. You could get a massage for what it would cost you to miss a day of work (and possibly a doctor's visit and meds on top of that).

Immune System

Did you know that massage has been shown to help increase the cells that fight breast cancer? Massage stimulates the flow of lymph, which is the body's natural defense system. Studies have shown an increase in killer T-cells and white blood cells after a massage, which help to fight off cancer cells and other harmful viruses in your body — good for overall immune support and keeping you free from illness.

Pain

Massage can help to alleviate pain and decrease the need for medications for migraine sufferers. Surprisingly, it can also shorten the length of labor for expectant mothers in addition to lessening anxiety and depression that commonly follows.

Circulation

Increases in circulation means more nutrients and oxygen to every cell in your body. This equates to increased recovery after exercise, increases in energy, increased focus and increased health.

In addition, massage has been shown to increase joint flexibility and range of motion, increase the recovery time from injury and lessen back and arthritis pain. Rather than going on and on about the benefits of massage, I'm going to go schedule one myself. I hope you reward yourself with one as well, for its benefits go beyond just the immediate relief and pleasure it provides. It's an important tool to keeping your body in optimum health.

"Laughter is an instant vacation."
—*Milton Berle*

FOR THE LOVE OF LAUGHTER

Life sometimes gets overwhelming for us, and the stress and sorrow we have to deal with can wear on our bodies and minds. We also can get so caught up with work that we don't take time to enjoy life or to just simply relax enough to laugh. When is the last time you saw a funny movie, read a joke that made you laugh or just had a fun time with laughing with friends? If you had to really think about it, and can't remember when you had a good laugh last, then a prescription for laughter is just what you need.

Laughter is beneficial to both physical and emotional health — it strengthens the immune system, helps keep blood vessels healthy and lowers stress and blood pressure.

Laughing causes an increase in oxygen intake, which enriches your heart, lungs and muscles — aiding in muscle relaxation, and in decreasing pain as well. When you laugh, the brain releases "feel-good" chemicals that help counteract stress hormones — providing a long-lasting mood boost and a natural treatment for anxiety and depression.

Did you know that laughter can also help improve memory?

A study of adults in their 60s and 70s measured levels of stress and short-term memory. One group sat quietly, while the other group watched funny videos. In comparing memory recall abilities afterwards, the humor group had an astonishing 43.6% success rate compared to 20.3% in the non-humor group. In addition, the humor group had significantly lower levels of the stress hormone cortisol.

Need help getting laughter in your life? Watch funny videos and movies, or share funny jokes and pics with others. Spend time with family or friends. Exercising in a group setting is also great idea — it's not only fun but provides much needed social interaction.

We all need to laugh — to keep laughter in our own lives and to provide it for others that so desperately need it.

Laughter will improve the quality of your life (in mind, body and spirit) and the lives of others as well. Laughter is one of the greatest anti-stressors there is. It helps us connect with others and heal physically and emotionally. Laughter, it truly is the best medicine— providing free refills for a long and happy life.

Mind Over Muffin Top Tip

Want to lose weight? Try this exercise. Turn your head to the right, then turn it to the left. Repeat the exercise after every time you are offered something to eat.

"Balance is not something you find, it's something you create."
—*Jana Kingsford*

BETTER BALANCE

What does balance mean to you? Standing on one leg? Being able to juggle work, family and getting the kids to their activities? Or feeling an inner peace within yourself? For most people, when it comes to their lives and feeling balance, I feel like they tend to try and juggle too many things at once. We can often feel like we're being pulled in multiple directions and feel stressed, frustrated, tired and truly out of balance. This can happen easily, as one can find themself spending more time on things that aren't important to them versus spending more time on the things that are. I often hear others say, "I need to find some balance." They struggle daily with juggling their schedules, and their life feels completely out of balance.

We are not all master jugglers and can only juggle so many things in our life at once.

So just how do you create this balance and become the master juggler you feel you need to be?

Evaluate and Assess

Think about what's really important to you in your life. Your family? Health? Career? Sit down and look at how you're spending your time. Write out what a typical week looks like for you for everything you do — work, travel time, socializing, exercise, watching TV, grocery shopping, cooking, etc.

Ask yourself if there is anything you can change to help create more balance.

For me, it was adjusting my work schedule so I can work out in the morning, and free up more time in the evening. Be honest with yourself in how you spend your time, and assess the need for change.

Want to exercise more and spend time with friends? Instead of going home straight to your couch after work, consider joining a friend for weekly walks or an exercise class instead. Perhaps you have a goal to reduce stress — you could schedule regular massages, plan quiet time for yourself to read or practice yoga.

It's just as important to keep these goals in mind as it is to accomplish the "must dos" in your weekly schedule.

Balance comes in many forms. Internally, it's in mind, spirit and health. Externally, it's in your work, family, friends and enjoyable activities. When you place value on achieving balance in all of these areas, then true happiness, peace and health can all be achieved. Create balance in yourself and your life, and a better life and a better you will be created in return.

Mind Over Muffin Top Activity

What does balance look like for you?

What could you accomplish if your life was more balanced?

What are specific actions you can take to achieve balance in your life?

"If you do not make time for your wellness, you will be forced to make time for your illness."
—*Joyce Sunada*

MASTER YOUR TIME, MASTER YOUR LIFE

Having a hard time fitting fitness into your life? I hear so many people say they have no time to exercise or that they don't have time to cook, but they seem to have the time to sit in a drive-thru line and update their Facebook status. I find that most people really do have the time, it's just a matter of not wasting it. There is time, and I'm going to help you find it.

Get Organized

Being unorganized is a huge time waster. If you spend an extra five minutes digging through your sock drawer trying to find a match every morning, that's time wasted. Whether it's trying to find an important document, your keys when you're running late or a tool you need that you misplaced — they are all a big waste of time. When you're more organized, you minimize the amount of time you waste. Taking the time to organize will save you a lot of time overall.

Manage Time Wisely

Using time wisely is crucial to creating balance in our lives and maximizing the time we need for ourselves. This is something I didn't do very well years ago, and I remember it quite well. On a section of my 4th grade report card, I was quite shocked to see that the teacher gave me a "Needs Improvement" score. I had thought I was doing well in school and was puzzled to what it could have meant. I read it more closely and saw that it was a section in the report card that the teacher rated the student's ability to use time wisely. Hmm, I guess the teacher didn't think taking naps or goofing off during our homework breaks was using time wisely. It made me think about it, and I guess she was right. If I did my homework during those breaks, it would be a much better use of my time, and then I would have more time to do whatever I wanted after school. I wanted to get better scores on that, so I buckled down and did it. Thanks for the valuable life lesson teach!

Now, I find myself doing much better with using my time wisely and feel like I have a lot more balance in my life because of it. For example, I like to watch a few TV shows in the evening to unwind, but I use that time in a productive way. I don't just sit on the couch and waste precious time; I stretch and foam roll while I watch my shows. With grocery shopping, I try and plan fewer and larger purchases so I don't have to shop as often. A lot of people make the mistake of running to the grocery store for a few items several times a week, and it ends up costing them a lot more time overall.

Prioritize and Plan

Each week, create a goal list of the things you want to accomplish. Using your weekly schedule, plan and schedule what is most important to you first. Planning ahead helps to ensure you accomplish your goals. If you just have it "in mind" that you need to work out this week, it's less likely to happen versus if you have set days and times that you plan to go. It will help you to be mentally prepared and motivated and manage your entire week better as well.

Prioritize and plan what's most important and has to be done first, and the rest will easily follow.

It's not about having the time, it's about your health not being a priority — it shouldn't be optional. It doesn't take a lot of time to reap the rewards and benefits that exercise provides. Even as little as 20–30 minutes a day can improve your health and fitness levels tremendously. Something is better than nothing at all. No time to exercise? I think not.

You can learn to master your time, and in turn master your life.

Mind Over Muffin Top Activity

Look at how you're spending your time and think of ideas to help save it. There is time, we just have to learn to how to use better.

What are things you would like to do but feel you do not have the time for?

Estimate how much time per day you spend doing the following:

Watching television =
Texting =
Facebook/Internet =
Email =

What do you spend the most time on?

How can you reduce the amount of time spent on this?

Do you feel a need to cut back on the other areas as well?

If so, what steps can you take to accomplish this?

"Do it now. Sometimes later becomes never."
—*Unknown*

BE A POSITIVE "UN-PROCRASTINATOR"

When feeling overwhelmed, think of things that can be done versus what cannot be done. Ask yourself, what is one thing I can do right now? The key is to try and do *something*, as there is usually something you can accomplish versus not doing anything. You may feel like you're helping yourself when you allow yourself not to do something, but the reality is that you're doing the exact opposite. By continually putting things off, you are putting more things on an already long list of "to do's."

Crossing things off your "to do" list will help reduce stress and induce a more positive mindset.

I used to be the "Queen of Procrastination." My dad's philosophy — "Why do today what you can put off until tomorrow?" It's funny, I was taking after my father and constantly adding things to a never ending to do list. Initially, it would feel like I was helping myself, but in the long run it created more stress and left me feeling overwhelmed.

Now, I try my best not to put things off, and I hope you will do the same. Pay that bill when it comes, schedule that doctor appointment you've been putting off or that oil change your car needs. The things you can't do right away, schedule a day and time to ensure it gets done. Use a planner, calendar or set reminders in your phone. It's time to stop putting things off, and start doing. It's time to be a positive "un-procrastinator" instead.

"The difference between a goal and a dream is a deadline."
—Steve Smith

PUTTING THE "GO" IN GOALS

Why is goal setting so important? Without a goal, there is no "go," and nothing to motivate you to take action. If you're overweight and unhealthy, and don't have a goal to lose weight, it's just not going to happen. When there is no "go" or desire to do such a thing, your health will likely deteriorate because of it.

Goals help develop motivation and give you that "go"— the fuel and drive to achieve.

When it comes to setting your goals though, there are key concepts that play a vital role.

Start Small

The road to success starts with taking small steps and starting with one goal versus trying to change too many things at once. Focus on what's most important to you, and start there. What are the steps needed to achieve your goal? Break them down into small achievable steps, and set a timeline for yourself. If you dream of running a marathon, start with a goal of running a 5k and work your way up. Every marathon runner had to start somewhere; they just didn't come out of their mothers' wombs running. Think baby steps before leaps and bounds.

The success of achieving the small goals will lead to the bigger success of achieving your bigger, long-term goals.

Think Smart

To help keep you on track, make your goals personal and S.M.A.R.T — specific, measurable, achievable, realistic and timely (have a completion date). With goals, it is important not to be vague but to have specific actions you want to do. For example, instead of a general goal of eating healthier, it could be to eat a bowl of oatmeal for breakfast instead of your typical donut.

Goals that are measurable would be something that you can track or monitor the progress of, like walking distance or time walked.

Be realistic with your goals. They need to be truly achievable in a realistic and reasonable time frame. Setting unrealistic and unachievable goals will only set yourself up for disappointment and discouragement.

Mind Over Muffin Top Tip

Have a catchy name for your goal to help keep it in mind. Use words that inspire and motivate you. For example, a goal to get in better shape by your 60th birthday could be called *My Super Sixty Plan.*

"The best motivation always comes from within."
—*Michael Johnson*

FINDING YOUR WHY

What good are goals if you can't stay on track and stay motivated? Being motivated takes getting to the heart of your goal and finding your why. AND most importantly, it takes having the right mindset. It is a matter of being ready for change, and wanting and believing that you can achieve it.

Having a positive mindset will serve a protective function, like a protective "roof" over the goals you want to achieve.

A negative mindset is like having a leaky roof, as it will erode away at your foundation and the pillars (your diet and exercise plan).

The Why Factor

It's very important to remember the whys, as in why you want to accomplish your goals. Your "why factor" should be what really drives you, what that burning desire in your heart really is. Finding that "why" is the desire that ignites that internal fire. It's the fire and desire you need to motivate yourself into action.

Goals give you that "go," and "whys" are the fire and fuel to achieve it.

For example, take a general goal like weight loss. Do it because you want to be healthier, because you want to be able to play with your kids or grandkids, or to be able to move and function better as you age. Keep your why in mind, because the more you really want and keep that in mind, the more likely you are to start making the changes you need.

Michelle's Story

Her #1 motivation: she doesn't want to end up like her parents. "Their health is not good. They went from being two active people, to just stopping all together. It makes me sad." Another thing that motivated Michelle was to build self-confidence. "My whole life I based my self-worth on my size, as my weight would go up, my self-confidence would go down." Michelle has struggled with body dysmorphia and had a few bouts with anorexia. To this day she still fights the urge to go back to that style of body control. "At my thinnest, I thought I looked awesome, but literally everyone else thought I was sick."

Michelle feels she is just one of many women who feel and deal with the same body image issues. She has been working hard to focus on just being a healthy person, for the sake of just being healthy. "I love and need exercise every day. I live to play! I just want to be able to keep rocking and rolling 'til the day I die. I don't want to ever be sidelined, and I want to be able to play with my future grandkids!"

Michelle has been working on slowly changing habits and her mindset to a healthier way of thinking and being. Her mindset and health have both grown in positive ways. Michelle's competitive nature keeps her determined to win and achieve her goals. It's no surprise to hear her say, "Some days it's hard, but I won't give up!"

Mind Over Muffin Top Activity

My philosophy with goals is that there are 5 components, the 5 Ws to ask yourself when setting them. This is a way to put your S.M.A.R.T. goals into action and to help develop a plan to stay on track.

What?   Be specific with your goals. What do you want to achieve? What do you need to achieve your goal? Remember to start with small achievable goals. Do you need to get a gym membership? Purchase running shoes? Hire a personal trainer?

When?   When do you want to accomplish these goals by? Reminder: be realistic with the time frame.

Where?   Will the actions you be taking to achieve your goal be at home, work or the gym? Where will the changes you are making take place? What is the location of your goal? Is there anything you can do to help you in that location/environment? Do you need to clear out any space at home? Does your kitchen need to be cleaned or organized?

Why?   Explain why your goal is important to you. Why do you want to achieve your goal? Keep asking why, until you feel you really get to the heart of your goal.

Whoa?   What are your "whoas" — the things that happen that typically derail you with staying on track with your goals? Do you often get off track when you stay up too late? Run out of food at home?

"Motivation is motive in action."
—Denis Waitley

MASTERING MOTIVATION

I love the start of the new year, for it is a time when it seems that almost everyone I know and encounter seems to be more motivated and trying to change for the better. They are working out, dieting and trying to improve their health. Most, I say, because the funny thing is that my father would be the exception. To him, he would say that another year going by is another nail in his coffin. Then I always think to myself, wouldn't you want to work on getting those nails out of your coffin? While others start tying up their shoelaces to head to the gym, my father is sliding on his slippers and heading for the couch. Sorry dad, you just came to mind as a good example.

How can you keep up the continued action that will help you not only achieve your goals at the beginning of a new year, but any goal you set for yourself throughout the year?

What is going to help you slide on those gym shoes and go to the gym versus putting on those slippers and heading to the couch?

Accountability

Want to increase your rate of success? Tell your friends, family and coworkers of the goals you have for yourself. Even better — find a workout buddy. Studies have shown that people who have workout "buddies" are more consistent with their fitness routines and get better results. Having someone you can meet up with to walk, run or take a class with will help provide support for the changes that you are trying to make. I think we all could benefit from someone keeping us accountable.

Whether it's a training coach, friend, or support group, being accountable to someone helps you stay on track. The biggest reason I see people fall off track is the lack of accountability. Most people aren't going to as accountable to themselves versus having a training coach or someone encouraging and helping them stay on track. It's normal to fall off track a little (and for some a lot). Being accountable to someone will likely help you get back on track versus getting totally derailed.

Vision

The key with goals is to have a vision of success, as it creates hope. With hope and vision, you create a picture of success. You take the belief of what you want to achieve and help make it a reality. If you don't believe you can do something, you likely won't achieve it. Vision gives us hope and increases the likelihood of achieving it. Just keep the picture of success realistic, and let it develop in your mind. Our mind can't tell the difference between what we think versus what we see. Program it for success; your mind wants to make things happen.

Vision boards are a great way to keep your goals in mind. Cut out motivational quotes and pictures that remind you of your goal and what you want to accomplish. Before I ever competed in bodybuilding, I created a collage poster of pictures of female bodybuilders I was inspired by, along with motivational sayings. You can also look up motivational quotes and images online and save them to your desktop,phone or print them out to post at home or work. Keep your goals and vision in mind every day, in everything you do. Are there movies that inspire, uplift and motivate you? Make a point to watch them when you find yourself struggling. Because when you keep your vision to believe and achieve, you will!

Put it in Writing!

Written goals help to clarify, commit and keep you accountable — it's key in helping you to focus on achieving them. There is something about writing down your goals that allows for it to stick more into your subconscious mind. In doing so, it helps make the visions of our goals believable, like bringing a blurry picture into focus. No more fuzzy and out of focus goals!

It's too easy to forget your goals if you don't have them written down. Maybe you have a goal of running in your first race — register, start training and make it happen.

Signing up for a race or competition is also a great way of literally putting your vision of that goal in writing, for your signature is committing you to your goal.

Schedule It

Get a calendar or planner and use it specifically for scheduling and planning your workout days and what you're going to do. When it's written down, and you see it, you're more likely to stick to doing it. Even better, choose a motivational calendar so you get an added dose of motivation. Like the well-known saying, "If you fail to plan, you plan to fail."

Celebrate wins

When you accomplish your goals, reward yourself. You want to reinforce the positive changes you're making, to help with that positive momentum and keep your motivation high. Achieve a goal of cutting back on smoking? Achieve a goal of walking on your lunch breaks? Celebrate! Take yourself out to a movie, treat yourself to a massage or go have lunch with a friend. Even if it's just doing a celebratory dance, it's something to acknowledge your efforts and progress. In the process of writing this book, every time I completed a chapter and printed it, I did a celebratory dance. It helped keep me going, made it much more enjoyable and I burned a few extra calories as well.

Turn on the Tunes

Research has shown that music has been successfully used to improve moods and overall happiness. Music increases the release of dopamine, which regulates motivation and goal-oriented behavior. Music has energizing effects and helps give you that extra spark. Music motivates

— whether it's to help you go for a walk, go to the gym or even just to cook dinner. When you listen to music, it will help make what you're doing more enjoyable, therefore making you more likely to do it. When I walk with headphones on and listen to my favorite songs, I walk twice as far as I do without it. Guess what kind of music I like to play when I clean? Polka! I find it fun and upbeat, and it makes the chore of cleaning much more pleasurable.

"We are what we repeatedly do. Success is not an action, but a habit."
—Aristotle

CREATING HABITS FOR SUCCESS

There are things we all want to do, goals we want to accomplish and things we want to change and improve on with ourselves. So, why is it that a lot of what we want to do and change just doesn't happen?

I'm no different than anyone else and have my struggles with that as well. A little secret about myself — I have a weakness for peanut butter, and I can tend to eat a little too much of it. One day I made a goal for myself to cut back on peanut butter. I decided to ditch my usual breakfast of peanut butter and jelly on brown rice cakes and switch it up to something a little heartier and healthier. Rice cakes aren't the problem, it's the three tablespoons of peanut butter and jelly I'm having with them, as they are a bit high in calories and sugar.

Did I do it, and make steel cut oatmeal like I planned on? Absolutely not, and I had a little peanut butter on the corner of my mouth as evidence. I even planned on cooking the oatmeal the night before, so all I would have had to do was pop it in the microwave that morning. I thought about it, but didn't do it.

I was successful at this before, so why was it so hard for me to make this simple change? I really enjoy eating it and how great I feel afterwards. I add in some fresh fruit, a scoop of my favorite vanilla protein powder and a handful of walnuts. It's an amazing supercharged breakfast of champions. It's not that my rice cake breakfast is all that bad, it's the fact that it's one of many things I have wanted to change but haven't.

So why didn't I accomplish my goal and make this simple change?

Why do people in general have such a hard time with simple changes?

We are creatures of habit. With a lot of our behaviors, we just go through the motions and are more or less on autopilot. In order to change, we need to escape from the bad habits we have.

Bad habits hijack our train to "Successville" and hijack our happiness with it.

BUT you can win the fight and learn how to stay on track with achieving your goals. It's a matter of understanding your habits, why you have them, and working towards creating better ones.

Habits are like grooves, like the grooves in a record. The more we repeat them, the deeper the etching in the groove becomes. When we try and start a new habit, we are in essence starting a new groove. It takes frequency and repeating that new behavior over and over to develop the new grooves we need to form new habits.

With consistency, the new habit will develop just like the grooves from the bad habits did.

Once we develop new habits, they will replace the old ones and become more of what feels automatic to us. It just takes time and patience. The more we do it, the easier it will become. In time, our new healthy behaviors will become habits and replace the bad ones. New daily habits become the new grooves of healthier habits.

What makes a new habit easier to start? Start small.

The goal is to achieve small, sustainable steps. Micro actions are the best way to start, for even as little as those every day actions may seem, they will add up and keep you moving towards achieving your goals.

When focusing on habits, do not focus on the result itself, but on making the changes that will lead to the result you want.

The 4 Rs of habit change we need to focus on: realistic, reminder, routine and reward.

Realistic — We need to be honest with ourselves as to what we feel we can realistically do.

Example — If you've been drinking a 2 liter of pop a day, it's doubtful you can just quit cold turkey and not drink any at all. It would be more realistic to work on cutting back on the amount you drink every day.

Reminder — Something that will trigger and remind you of what you want to do.

Example — setting a reminder on your phone to drink a glass of water throughout the day.

Routine — An action you can do on a consistent basis.

Example — drink a glass of water in the morning before you drink your coffee.

Reward — When you accomplish your new behaviors, you want to reward yourself for the changes you've made.

Example — You accomplished your goal of walking on your lunch every day this week, so you treat yourself to a movie over the weekend.

Look at your current behaviors. Think about them and if they're in tune with leading you to the results you want. If you are training for a marathon and have a diet of junk food, it's not going to give you the necessary fuel your body needs to train. Remember, you do not have to change all your behaviors at once.

Change is about giving up less important things for the ability to achieve the bigger, more important goals.

Is it more important to lose weight and reduce your chances of a heart attack or to keep having that donut every morning?

85% of behavior change is what you bring to the table — experience, knowledge, abilities and the ability to recognize thoughts. All of these are things you can increase and improve on, helping you to be successful in making the changes you want. One habit at a time, one change at a time and one day at a time — you can make the changes that will lead you to success.

Mind Over Muffin Top Activity

What are your current habits? Do you smoke, drink pop, eat fast food, skip breakfast? What kind of exercise routine do you have? How long have you been doing it for? Take a serious look at your lifestyle and your habits, even better, write them down. Prioritize the things you would like to change first. If it's easier, you can choose to work on one thing at a time. If you try to change everything at once, it could be too overwhelming. Habits are hard to break, so be patient with yourself. It takes several weeks to break a habit, but only one to start. Let's make it the start of a new, healthier habit.

List your bad habits:

How can you improve on the bad habits that you have?

What healthy habits can you start doing? Remember to keep it realistic.

What reminders can you put in place for yourself?

Kate's Story

Sitting in a ski lodge in Colorado, she told herself, "I'm done with being overweight and unhealthy." It was December 2016, and her weight had climbed to an all-time high of 247 lbs. Once athletic and fit, she now found herself getting out of breath on the ski slopes and not able to keep up with the rest of her family. "I was finally ready to do something about it. I wasn't going to spend the rest of my life dragging around on the sidelines."

Growing up, Kate played sports all year long and managed to stay in great shape. "Into my late twenties, I did ok. If my clothes started to get snug, I would get out and exercise and I'd drop 5 or 10 lbs. But when I reached my 30s, it didn't work anymore." With two young children, Kate was gaining more and more weight. "I was diagnosed with depression and hypothyroidism, and while medication helped, it didn't get rid of the extra pounds I gained."

For the next 15 years she rode the yo-yo up and down. "I tried exercising more, only to have the weight boomerang back the moment I stopped. I tried different diets but couldn't keep up with it all. Nothing seemed sustainable." Kate became overwhelmed and finally quit trying. She missed her old athleticism and had resigned to being that "cute but chubby" girl, destined to watch life from the sidelines. By the time Kate turned 49 in July 2016, she weighed in at her heaviest ever: 247 lbs.

"Later that year I was at my doctor's office after hurting my knee. I saw "morbidly obese" written on my chart, and I thought, "Yikes!" Then, after skiing that winter, and finding myself huffing and puffing while my family charged ahead, I said, "That's it!" That's when I decided to embark on my "Fit by 50" journey."

Inspired by a friend's success, Katie called her and told her to sign her up. She dove 110% into a lifestyle and nutrition transformation program. "Within days, I had so much energy — my brain fog lifted, I regained clarity and focus and I felt alive again! I learned to think of food as fuel for my body, to enjoy exercise and how to build healthier habits that would support these changes: sleep, hydration, mindfulness, supportive relationships and personal growth — all of these necessary components for building real and lasting change."

Kate went on to lose 101 pounds, reaching 146 lbs. in November. "The real miracle lays on the inside, on the intangibles you can't see, weigh or measure. I gained so much more than the weight I lost: inner confidence, freedom, strength, tons of energy, real health, renewed hope, new friends and JOY!"

Kate is now a full-time health coach, and instead of sitting on the sidelines feeling tired and depressed, she wakes up each morning with a sense of purpose, hope and fulfillment: ready to go out and help others find their freedom too. "My 50s are turning out to be my best decade yet!"

"Tomorrow you promise yourself will be different, yet
tomorrow is often a repetition of today."
—James T. McCay

WHY WAIT?

How many times have you told yourself you would start doing something tomorrow, yet repeated the same behaviors of yesterday? Maybe it is a promise to quit smoking, to start exercising or to eat healthier.

Think about behaviors you have been wanting to change and how long you have been wanting to change them. For most of us, they are behaviors we have been wanting to change for a long time. Have you started making any changes to improve your health? How much longer are you going to put them off?

When are you going to break the cycle of repeating yesterday's behavior?

Week after week, I told myself I was going to switch from drinking coffee to tea. I even woke up one morning thinking of that quote, and ironically, about making a pot of coffee as well. I told myself, "I can start tomorrow." Sure, I could promise myself that, but I had already been doing that the past several weeks. Being that I found myself wanting to put it off again, I realized I was guilty of wanting to repeat yesterday's behavior. I thought about my goals and the behaviors I wanted to change. I thought to myself — today was the time, not tomorrow, to start making those changes. I said yes to my goals, yes to the tea, and no to the coffee.

The last thing one wants to do is put off getting started. There is always something you can do and something that you can start now. By reading this book you already are. Good job! But of course, you can do a little more (or hopefully a lot more). It could be as simple as making a grocery list, finding some recipes you want to try or scheduling times to exercise in your planner. At least it is something, and that something can be a life-changing, fire-starting spark. That spark is exactly what is needed to start the fire of motivation, the fire we want to keep forever burning.

Stop making bad choices and stop putting things off. Once you initially break that repetitious cycle, it is much easier to repeat the new behavior.

If you want to have a better tomorrow, you have to make better choices today.

Healthy choices develop healthy habits. Those healthy choices can start today. Bad choices today can limit your tomorrows, limit your life and the quality in which you live it. Make a choice today, to not only give you a better tomorrow, but more of them.

Mind Over Muffin Top Activity

What are things you want to change but have been putting off?

What are things you can do to help motivate you to change them?

What will help make it easier for you to make these changes?

"Faith is taking the first step even when you don't see the whole staircase."
—*Martin Luther King, Jr.*

TAKE THAT FIRST STEP

What's the hardest part about achieving a goal? It's getting started and taking that first step. But more than that, it's believing and having faith that you can achieve that goal. If you fail to believe, you fail to start. Just believing you can do something helps ignite the fire of motivation that is so crucial in the mental preparation it takes to create action.

Sometimes we feel like we have such a difficult climb, that it's unachievable. All you have to do is take a step — start walking, join a gym, enroll in an exercise class — just do it. In taking a step you're moving forward, and you're one step closer than you were before.

You'll never get to the top of the staircase and achieve your goals unless you take the steps to get there.

You may not see the top of the staircase or be able to see what you can achieve, but have faith that you will get there. Believe in the fact that one day you will be at the top of that staircase and be able to look down and see how far you've come. Believe it and you can achieve it.

Take a step today, do something that will get you one more step closer to the goals you want to achieve.

Do it today, and don't let another day go to *waist* (or your behind). One healthy step forward is better than an unhealthy step backward — and better than not taking a step at all.

Mind Over Muffin Top Activity

Let's put that "believe and achieve" vision into action and embed it in your mind. With each of your goals, journal as if you have already accomplished them. Write down how it feels, what you experience and all the amazing things that come with it. This is a powerful way to program our minds for success.

"Life has no remote, you have to get up and change it yourself."
—*Mark Cooper*

CHANGE THE CHANNEL

Tired of feeling tired? Not sleeping well? Or perhaps you have a nagging back or knee pain that you just can't seem to recover from. A recent work training I attended involved an activity in which each participant had to state something they weren't happy about. I was shocked and saddened to hear the alarming number of people that complained of back pain, knee pain, lack of sleep or were unhappy with their weight. I would estimate that about 80% of the them had some sort of physical complaint.

After this, we were each then told to make a positive comment about the thing we were unhappy about. I noticed that the positive statements involved that person knowing that they can do something about it. Statements like: "I'm overweight, but I can start exercising and feel better," "I can go see a doctor about my back," and "I can go do a sleep study."

Unfortunately, it often takes pain and suffering for us to make a change. Things have to get bad enough to finally motivate us to make a change.

You can't expect to see a change if you don't make one.

It seems that people just wait for the chance that they'll just feel better, have more energy, be pain free and lose weight. I really wish that could happen for people, but the reality is that it won't. It will be a matter of changes being made, not by chance.

If you want a different result, you need to start making different choices.

It's quite possible that your back and knee pain may just be where your pain is presenting, while tight or weak muscles, or a combination of the two, are usually the actual culprits. For example, if you sit for too many hours a day, the hip flexors and hamstrings can become tight and pull on your hips, which in turn pulls on your back. Not sleeping at night? It could be anxiety, stress or an overconsumption of caffeine. Feeling tired all the time? Most often it's a matter of inactivity or a poor-quality diet.

We need to get to the root cause of our pain and problems, and try to do something proactive to resolve it.

You can start cutting back on your coffee intake, start a walking program, take that yoga class or start eating healthier. We can't push a button on a remote to change, but we can push ourselves to do something about it. Hopefully, I've pushed *your* buttons enough to do so!

Mind Over Muffin Top Activity

What does your current channel of "Health and Fitness" look like? Does it show you walking, eating healthy, riding your bike with friends, doing yoga, cooking healthy meals, looking happy and full of life? Or does it show you watching a lot of television, eating junk food, walking around stiff and sore and looking stressed and tired?

Imagine you had a remote control and could press a button to change the channel.

What do you want that "New You" channel to look like?

What are you doing in that "New You" channel?

Keep what that "New You" channel looks like in your mind, and think of how amazing it will feel to star live in it every day.

What changes do you need to make to be that healthier person?

What steps can you take today to start implementing those changes and make it a reality?

"It is health that is real wealth, not just pieces of gold and silver."
—*Mahatma Gandhi*

FOR THE HEALTH OF IT

I'm sure we've all done things "for the heck of it," but why not more for the health of it? Why do we wait for something to hurt, for us to feel sick, or get to the point of having a serious health issue before we decide to make a change and do something that's good for us? Most people do more preventative measures and take better care of their car than they do for their own bodies.

Our health is just like a car, in that when it starts showing signs that it's in need of repair, it can get more costly to ignore at that point.

The damage often gets worse and will come with a higher repair bill than if we had it fixed right away. The price tag on repairing a human body when it breaks down is much more expensive.

On top of that, you're feeling the symptoms, feeling the aches and pains and having to live with a broken-down body. Ever consider the cost of meds and medical care that you will incur if and when your body breaks down? It comes with a much higher price tag then giving your body the preventative care it needs. People often have prescription meds that cost them several hundreds of dollars a month and medical bills on top of that. In addition, think of all the time someone would have to spend in doctors' offices and hospital.

All too often, people don't have a clue to the damage they're doing to their bodies until it has progressed to the point of disease.

Usually by the time someone experiences symptoms, that person could already be at the point where not only their health, but their life is at serious risk. For example, high blood pressure and high cholesterol are a few common culprits to heart disease. You can't feel high cholesterol, and you typically can't feel high blood pressure. BUT you can feel chest pain, which could be the sign of a heart attack.

The status of your health is a result of the choices you have made. If you eat a high-fat diet, don't exercise, abuse alcohol, smoke, etc., you will end up paying the price for it by suffering from poor health, disease and a decreased quality of life.

Just like a car will break down if you don't care for it, your body will break down as well.

BUT guess what, you can greatly improve your health and decrease the risk of disease by eating healthier and exercising! High cholesterol and high blood pressure can often be eradicated with proper nutrition and exercise. Diabetes, heart disease, cancer, you name it — all possibly eliminated through healthy lifestyle changes.

What you gain from making positive changes is far better than continuing to slide downhill with your health and fitness levels.

If you make healthy choices, if you CHOOSE to take care of your body and give it the preventative care it needs, you can avoid many health complications down the road.

Not only that, you will feel better, live better and you will be better. A healthy body is a happy body, and with a happy body comes a happy life.

Get started today and do something for the "health of it"!

I was inspired to write about this topic after I got a computerized body scan at my chiropractor's office, which pinpointed areas of my body that were determined to be "unhealthy" or at risk. What stood out the most was my heart and high blood pressure. Having this in-depth look into my body made me take a deep look into myself. It made me think of how important it was for me, and for everyone, to really think about all the choices they make when it comes to the health of their body.

I was lucky enough to have this scan and to be made aware of it. It made me realize that I needed to address the results so I wouldn't end up having serious health problems down the road. Could I cut back on the amount of beer I was drinking? Yes. Was I slacking in the amount of cardio I was doing? Yes. Did I need to improve the quality of my sleep? Yes. Did I need to manage my stress better? Yes. I made a vow to improve on all of those things, and I did.

Mind Over Muffin Top Activity

Would you like to be healthier?

Think of the changes you want to make. Write down what you want to change.

I want to _____

I want to _____

I want to _____

Focus on what you can change.

Can you smoke less? Drink more water? Eat more fruits and vegetables?

Write down what you can start changing.

I can _____

I can _____

I can _____

"The self is not something ready-made, but something in continuous formation through choice of action."
—*John Dewey.*

CHOOSING TO TAKE ACTION

How happy are you with the choices that you have made in your life? Think about it: where you are in your life at this very moment is a cumulative result of the choices that you have made over the course of your lifetime. It is more than location alone, it also includes your mental health, physical health, career, kids, the amount of money you have in the bank and so on. Is your health where you would like it to be? Are you in as good of shape as you want to be in?

Take a marathon runner for an example. Someone does not just go out and decide to run a marathon one day, as they must train for several months to complete such a feat. How do they start? It starts with a choice, a decision that they are going to commit to a training schedule that will allow them to achieve their goal. It is the accumulation of steps, the continual choice to run, again and again. From that continuous choice of action, a marathon runner is born. They might be born to run, but they certainly did not jump out of their mother's womb with running shoes on and start running.

Our days are filled with choices, and lots of them. We choose whether we get out of bed or hit the snooze button. We choose what we are going to wear, how fast we drive to work and if we are going to eat the donuts someone brought to work that day.

Think of all the many choices you have to make in one day and how you spend your time and energy. Is it in line with the goals you want to achieve for yourself? Are you happy with where you are at in your life? If running a marathon is a goal of yours, then you want to be sure to make choices that would allow you to have the time and energy to do so.

Focus on your goals and what choices you need to make to help you achieve them.

If you want to run a marathon, you will choose to get proper rest and not stay up late watching *The Late Show* every night. You will choose to eat healthy foods that fuel your training efforts — meaning you won't give in to tempting junk food at work and stick to your nutrition plan. After a stressful day, you will choose to stick to your training routine and workout after work and won't go home to the couch and potato chips calling your name. One step at a time and one choice at a time — you can create the you that you desire to be!

Mind Over Muffin Top Activity

Think of your goals and what you'll need to achieve them. The more you can do to prepare yourself for the changes you want to make, the better off you'll be and the better your chances of being successful. For example, let's say you want to eat healthier. Purchasing a cookbook with healthier recipes or looking up recipes online would be an action that is preparing yourself for the changes you want to make. Want to start exercising? Join a gym, find a workout buddy or purchase fitness attire to exercise in if needed.

What better choices can you start making today?

What steps can you take today to start yourself on a path to achieving your dream?

ASSESS AND ADDRESS FOR SUCCESS!

Like the physical homes that we live in, we have to be aware of and assess any issues we may have – cracks in the foundation, unstable pillars/walls, leaky roofs, etc. Just as we need to maintain the homes that we live in, we need to do the same with our bodies 'house' that we live in as well.

"We can now view our bodies 'house' in this way,
to keep in mind the key components of the foundation."

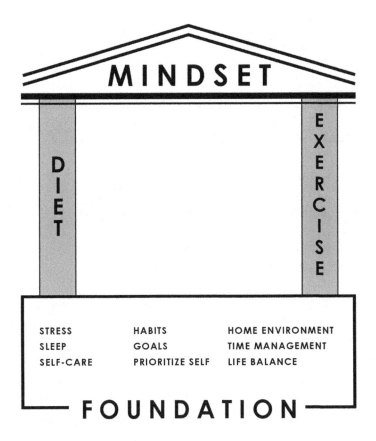

It will be important to be mindful and assess your foundation on a daily basis, and take corrective action as needed. Motivation wavers and declines with cracks in the foundation, and can start to erode away at the pillars (diet and exercise plan) if we aren't careful. When you start off with building a solid foundation, you start off on a solid track. And when you learn to 'assess and address' any problems you have along the way, you keep yourself on track. In essence, you can 'assess and address' for success!

'Assess and Address' any changes needed in these key areas of your foundation:

Stress Management — ability to effectively manage and reduce negative effects

Sleep — achieving an adequate amount of quality sleep on a consistent basis

Home Environment — amount of clutter, organizational needs, feng shui

Prioritize Self — saying yes to yourself, taking care of your needs first

Self-care — recognizing the need and ability to implement

Life Balance — ability to manage and maintain a sense of balance

Time Management — ability to implement and practice

Goals — finding your why, starting small, keeping it S.M.A.R.T.

Habits — ability to develop and sustain healthy habits

To keep your foundation strong, practice being mindful of how 'fit' your foundation is on a daily basis.

Once a week, go through this list and assess each area of your foundation. When you see a need for change or improvement, address it! Don't let things go or get out of control. This will help you to take corrective action as needed in a timely manner.

Doing so is vitally important to keeping yourself on track to make the continued progress needed to achieve your goals.

2

THE DIET PILLAR

"Let food be thy medicine, and they medicine by the food."
—Hippotcrates

THE DIET AND HEALTH CONNECTION

The diet pillar is what bears the most weight when it comes to our health and wellness. Our diet comprises everything we eat, drink and the supplements we take (if any). What we choose to put in our bodies has a great effect on us. It will either be nourishing or depleting, improving our health or weakening it.

The importance of a nutritious diet and making healthy choices shouldn't be overlooked.

It is the core element in optimal health and wellness, and as we age it becomes more important than ever to give your body the nutrients it needs.

Would you like ...

protection from chronic disease?

to be able to manage your weight better?

to improve the strength of your immune system?

to improve your mental and physical health?

You can do all of the above with a nutritious diet. The choice is in your hands and what you choose to put in your body.

We've become a nation of fast-food fanatics and pill poppers. It seems that people can't resist the dollar menu appeal to get their dollar fries, nuggets or the like. I've heard so many people say they buy food on the dollar menu because it's "affordable" to them, that they are on a tight budget. They have no real idea of the true cost that these foods have on them.

Then there's the plethora of pill popping. Have back pain? Pop a pill. Can't sleep? Pop a pill.

People look for a quick fix and want pills and medications to fix them, often without a thought to look for the root cause of the problem.

Take back pain for example, it's quite often a combination of tight hamstrings and poor posture. Popping a muscle relaxer or taking a pain pill is often only going to prolong, and often exacerbate the problem, as one isn't getting to the root cause to correct it.

People are writing the script for their health or disease by the everyday actions and choices they make.

Eating fast food on a regular basis? You're writing a script for high cholesterol, diabetes and heart disease. Then, once you're finally diagnosed with those conditions, what are you given? A prescription for a medication. Then often those medications cause side effects, and then you're given another prescription to manage that. In the long run: huge medical bills, costly meds and a lot of time spent trying to manage your health. Are those dollar fries really worth it now?

The cost they will have on your health is definitely not worth it.

Unfortunately, most medical doctors receive very little nutrition education in medical school. They are taught to diagnose and treat, which quite typically involves medications. They aren't prevention specialists or trained to give specialized nutritional advice. I'm a big believer in getting to the root cause of a problem or health issue and treating in as much of a holistic and naturopathic manner as possible. I am not advocating that people never take medications, as with certain medical conditions they can be absolutely critical.

It boils down to realizing that food can either heal or harm you. Quit choosing to ignore the fact that eating poorly is harmful. Let's learn how to heal and be healthy from the inside out.

"Every human being is the author of his own health or disease."
—*Buddha*

LIFESTYLE MEDICINE

Sometimes your diagnosis isn't an end all be all. Saray Stacic, M.D., is living proof of that. She received a debilitating diagnosis of MS and was told she was facing the inevitable physical decline that would land her in a wheelchair. Fast forward, and she not only conquered the amazing feat of running a marathon, but also got off ALL of her MS meds and beat her once bleak and dire prognosis. Her book, "What's Missing from Medicine," tells the story of this amazing doctor's journey from disease and desperation to one of health and happiness.

How did she do it? She changed her diet and lifestyle. Dr. Stancic became the patient of her own best treatment plan — lifestyle medicine.

In her book, she discusses the importance of lifestyle medicine, an evidence-based clinical discipline used to prevent, treat and reverse chronic diseases.

Through positive lifestyle behavior change, one can prevent and reverse many diseases and improve the quality of one's life.

It's a remarkable, eye opening and life-changing book.

In her book she talks about epigenetics, specifically the idea of predisposing genes for a particular disease. You have the power to control the switch, as you turn those genes off or on via the choices you make — your diet and lifestyle. Dr. Stancic just happened to stumble upon some studies linking diet and lifestyle to MS outcomes, and the rest is history.

She now lives an active and symptom-free life without having to take any medications for MS.

How amazing! I hope you take the time to read her inspiring story and to learn more about the significance of lifestyle change and the impact it can have on your life. It really can be a life saver!

Book — "What's Missing from Medicine: Six Lifestyle Changes to Overcome Chronic Illness" by Saray Stancic, MD

For more information, visit drstancic.com

"I cannot say whether things will get better if we change;
what I can say is they must change if they are to get better."
—Georg C. Lichtenberg

READY FOR CHANGE

Change. What does the word "change" mean to you? By definition it means to make or become different. But for a lot of people, just hearing the word often brings with it a sense of fear, a thought of, "Oh no, what's going to happen?" It invokes resistance, anger and frustration.

Why? It's how one looks at it, and it's often viewed in a negative light.

The biggest reason people resist change is because they tend to focus on what they have to give up, instead of what they have to gain.

When it comes to weight loss, I've found that right off the bat people think of all the things they need to give up and can't have anymore.

For example, I've had clients say these following things to me:

"I guess I can't have ice cream anymore."

"I assume I can't go out to eat anymore."

"I can't live without my chocolate."

These types of statements are quite typical and demonstrate the automatic response to change people often have. They feel they are going to have to give up things they like or not be able to do something they enjoy.

Why focus on the negative when there are so many more positives to gain?

Yes, change can involve having to give something up, but the reality is that what we are giving up is often not worthy of doing or having. Instead, we need to view change in the positive light that it really is and focus on what we will gain instead.

Try to view change as making a shift from one thing to another or undergoing a modification or transformation.

AND think of how much better your life can be and how much better you will feel.

Whether it's putting out that cigarette, cutting out the junk food or starting an exercise program, changes like these bring with it an increased quality of life and longevity. We have far more to gain than what we feel we are losing.

Take those previous statements for example:

"I guess I can't have ice cream anymore."

Think of it this way: you can have ice cream. A healthier version would be more ideal, or quite possibly you can find something else you enjoy eating for dessert that is better for you.

"I assume I can't go out to eat anymore."

You can go out to eat, it's what you choose when you go out to eat that may be the problem. You can learn how to make healthier choices.

"I can't live without my chocolate."

You don't have to live without it. There are several foods that will help with that chocolate craving. You may also find that you're craving sweets due to physiological reasons. When you start eating more balanced, your cravings may go away.

Change doesn't always mean giving things up, instead, think of it as doing things better.

Change is action, and it's more than often better for us than we think or fail to realize. The key is to focus on the positives and what you can gain.

You will have more energy, better health and increased focus and productivity — and I can go on and on.

Appreciate the positives to whatever it is you are trying to accomplish.

- Would you rather be stuck or make changes and see things change?
- Realize that there are some things you cannot change.
- Control what you can control.
- Work on the changes you can make.

Change can be uncomfortable and take us out of our comfort zone. But when we stay "comfortable," we often aren't pushing ourselves to change, and to change for the better. Don't wait for a crisis to make a change, take control of your life and start making changes today.

"There's no doubt that the key to good health lies in the gut."
—Dr. Will Bulsiewicz

THE FIBER FACTOR

Want to dramatically transform your health? Feel good from the inside out? It's simpler than you think, and it doesn't involve a restrictive diet. No fads here, it's all cutting-edge science known to promote weight loss, long term health, optimize your immune system, reduce food sensitivities, lower cholesterol, reverse type 2 diabetes, improve brain function and even prevent cancer. And guess what, you can do all of this through the power of fiber!

In his book, "Fiber Fueled," Dr. Will Bulsiewicz teaches us that by eating a fiber-rich diet — fruits, vegetables, whole grains, seeds, nuts and legumes — you can transform your life and improve your health beyond what you could ever imagine.

In his gastroenterology practice, Dr. Will discovered that his patients would see dramatic improvements in their health with improvements in their diet. It inspired and led him to do in-depth research on gut health and to write this amazing book and share his knowledge with the world.

This book provides eye-opening, immensely-educational and valuable information that is crucial for everyone's health and wellness.

Dr. Will teaches us that we need fiber-rich foods, from as many different types of foods as possible, and that elimination diets are too restrictive. Studies show that elimination diets are harmful to our gut health.

Gut health is needed for optimal metabolism, hormone balance and minimizing inflammation that is the culprit of multiple diseases.

Whether it's reading this book or just learning about gut health in general, I highly advise you to do so. You can transform your health and your life by optimizing the health of your gut. You can feel better than ever from the inside out!

WHAT'S YOUR GUT TELLING YOU?

Did you know that diet has a huge impact on our moods? Avoiding refined and processed foods is just as important for our moods as it is our health. A diet high in these foods can lead to increases in depression and mood swings. But on the flip side, if we get a balanced amount of complex carbohydrates and lean proteins in our diet, it can naturally increase serotonin levels (the feel-good chemicals in our brains).

Studies have shown that people whose diets were high in fruits, vegetables, unprocessed grains, fish and seafood, had 25–35% less risk of depression. Also, people whose diets were low in omega fats were six times more likely to suffer from depression.

A poor diet — high in sugar, refined carbs and saturated fats — causes inflammation and stress on our bodies, which in turn affects our gut health and our brain. If our gut health is compromised, the health of our body and mind is compromised.

Like a high-performance sports car, our brains function best on premium fuel.

You wouldn't put sugar in your car's gas tank, but we put that and other junk in *our* gas tanks and expect it to run smoothly. Putting junk in your body negatively impacts gut health, and in turn our serotonin levels.

Where is the majority of this serotonin made? Our gut! Our gut is where it's believed that 80% of our immune system resides, and what makes about 95% of our serotonin.

The state of our gut health is what dictates how we feel on a daily basis.

When our gut is damaged, or inflamed, it can make us feel sick and fatigued. Many brain disorders have been linked to alterations in the function of our gut health — depression, anxiety, autism spectrum disorders, Parkinson's disease and Alzheimer's.

Feeling down? Sick? Tired? What is your gut telling you? Start paying attention to how you feel after eating, noticing how each food makes you feel. Try using a food journal to track your how you feel physically and mentally for a few weeks, and note any negative patterns you notice. Be certain to note how you feel the day after as well, as some foods have a delayed effect.

"Your body is the most priceless possession. Take care of it."
—Jack Lalane

WONDERFUL WATER

Did you ever think that a lack of water could have an effect on your weight loss efforts? Or your energy levels? When you're dehydrated, your body stores more fat and has a huge negative impact on energy and strength levels.

It is really the most important and easiest thing for someone to do, but most people fail at getting the necessary amounts for their bodies to function optimally.

Water is necessary for life and all body functions. It is needed for energy metabolism, detoxification, digestion, blood pressure, muscle strength and endurance, your immune system and kidney function.

Most people head straight to the coffee pot or pop open a diet soda to try and get them going for the day. You are already starting your day in a somewhat dehydrated state because you don't drink anything in your sleep. Drinking caffeinated beverages causes your body to lose water because caffeine is a diuretic. On the other hand, if you start your day by hydrating with water first, you're less likely to get dehydrated during the day.

Get in the habit of drinking a large glass of water upon arising, and better yet, ice water.

It will help to hydrate your body and has an added bonus — drinking ice water will burn more calories because your body has to heat the water. Another tip: drink a glass of water before meals. It not only helps increase your water intake, but it can increase metabolism by 10–30%.

The general recommendations are to drink between a half-ounce to an ounce per pound that you weigh. If you live in a warmer climate and exercise frequently, it will be on the higher end. If you live in colder climate and are sedentary, the lower end.

Like the slogan from the old American Express commercial advised: "Don't leave home without it" — don't leave home without a water bottle. It will help you to drink more and keep your metabolism up as well.

Mind Over Muffin Top Activity

Take a before and after picture of your face. The "before" picture will be now, and the "after" picture will be after you make an effort to drink more water for one month. We'll let the pictures do the talking. I'm sure you'll be happy with the results.

"The food you eat can be either the safest and most powerful form of medicine or the slowest form of poison."
—Ann Wigmore

SUGAR — THE UNSWEET TRUTH

So, what's the big deal? Sugar can't be all that bad, or can it? How can something that tastes so good be bad for you?

One thing that most people don't know is that an increase in sugar weakens your immune system.

The effects can last up to several hours. Drinking pop all day can seem harmless, but what it is actually doing is keeping your body in a compromised state all day long. A bottle of pop may only cost a dollar, but think of the total cost it is creating on your overall health. A diet high in sugar can aggravate asthma, cause mood swings, provoke personality changes, cause diabetes, increase your risk of heart disease, increase blood pressure, increase your triglycerides and cholesterol, and increase fat stores. Think it is a big deal now? I sure hope so!

Can you guess how much the average American consumes in sugar each week? A frightening 2–3 lbs. a week. The American Heart Association's recommended daily amounts of sugar a day are a maximum of 30 grams for women and 45 grams for men. To put it in perspective, 1 teaspoon equals approximately 4.2 grams.

If you do the math, the average American is consuming 4–6 times more than the recommended amount of sugar.

A fifteen-year study on the correlation between added sugar and heart disease had some alarming results. It was found that those who took in 25% of their daily calories as added sugar were twice as likely to die from heart disease compared to those who kept their diets under 10% of added sugar. This was true despite the age, sex, activity level or weight of the participants.

Another study looked at how eating heart-healthy foods like fruits and veggies might help offset the damage of a high sugar intake. Despite having a high healthy eating index score (someone that had a high intake of fruits and vegetables), a high added sugar intake still was linked to higher cardiovascular mortality.

The odds of someone dying from heart disease rose in tandem with the percentage of sugar in their diet.

It's quite possible that you are unintentionally consuming sugar, as it is often in things we don't even think about — bread, cereal, mayonnaise, peanut butter, condiments and spaghetti sauce. It reminds me of the fact that I was doing it myself, in my use of ketchup. There used to be a hot sauce commercial that had an elderly lady admitting, "I put that stuff on everything." (This is an edited version of what she really said.) I used to compete in bodybuilding and would go on extremely strict diets which included eating a lot of chicken, vegetables and egg whites.

So, for me, it was ketchup — I would put "that stuff" on everything. It did not even dawn on me how much sugar it had in it. I was dumping sugar on my diet food without realizing it — no wonder I got colds a lot and had a hard time losing my belly. Fortunately, I now know to read nutrition labels and to think about the sugar content in everything I eat and drink.

To make it simple, I tell my clients to try and keep their sugar intake in the single digits, below 10 grams for everything they eat (of course the lower the better). It is a simple way to make sure you are not overdoing the sugar. Did you know an average 20-ounce bottle of pop contains 65 grams of sugar? That is more than double the amount of recommended sugar for a woman.

A diet high in sugar causes a lot of stress on your body. This can be in the form of added sugar or from consuming too many simple carbs. Simple carbs are refined carbohydrates and sugars: white bread, white rice, pop, pastries, cakesand cookies.

**All carbohydrates break down into sugar,
but not all carbs are bad for you.**

Complex carbs provide needed nutrients and fiber, whereas simple carbs do not. More on that later in the book. So, if you eat a huge plate of pasta, even though pasta itself is low in sugar, it has a high number of carbs that can result in higher sugar levels. An increase in sugar causes your pancreas to release insulin to drop the blood sugar. What typically happens is that your blood sugar will end up dropping too low, leaving you tired and craving sweets again.

This vicious cycle will not stop unless you stop choosing to consume these sugar-spiking foods.

Over time, sugar will wreak havoc on your body and can result in diabetes. Your body becomes resistant to the insulin, which can cause blood sugar levels to elevate even more so. Elevated blood sugar levels increase the fat in your blood, clogging your arteries and increasing your risk of heart attack and stroke. This is not something to take lightly. Your diet can be killing you, and you need to be aware of it. Avoid sweets — be sweet to yourself and kind to your body — for that is the best treat you can give yourself.

Mind Over Muffin Top Activity

- Look at the foods you have at home and the amount of sugar they contain.

- When shopping, start reading nutrition labels and look for lower sugar alternatives.

- Start tracking the amount of sugar you consume in a day.

*"The doctor of the future will no longer treat the human frame
with drugs, but rather cure and prevent disease with nutrition."*
—*Thomas Edison*

DIET AND INFLAMMATION

An alarming 70% of Americans are on some form of medication —
antibiotics, antidepressants and pain killers top the list. Quite typically,
when someone experiences symptoms such as pain, fatigue, or illness,
the first thing we want to do is take a pill for it. Whatever the symptom,
we have become a society of pill poppers and quite often forget to look
for the cause.

**Although medications may be medically necessary depending on
one's medical condition, one can often reduce or eliminate the need
for them by eliminating the root cause of their condition**.

What is the single common denominator of all this pain and suffering?
Chronic inflammation in our bodies, with the standard American diet
being the number one cause.

How does our diet cause inflammation? An excess of sugar and refined
carbohydrates is the main culprit.

**Not only does this high sugar intake cause an increase in
inflammation, but it can also increase your cholesterol as well.**

-Remember that bit of information from the last chapter on sugar?
Inflammation plus high cholesterol quite often equals heart disease. A

high-acidic diet will also cause an increase in inflammation — salt, white flour, dairy, meat and soft drinks. It is also especially important to stay away from trans fats and saturated fats, as these cause an inflammatory response in your body as well.

Why is this inflammation so bad? Every chronic disease is an inflammatory disease, and most Americans suffer from chronic inflammation that weakens one's health and ages you prematurely.

Heart disease, diabetes, Alzheimer's, asthma, obesity, cancer and arthritis — all have root causes from chronic inflammation in the body.

This chronic inflammation damages our bodies' DNA and overwhelms our immune system, aging us, causing disease, pain, illness and fatigue. Not many people think to take a close look at their diet if they are experiencing any of these problems.

What is the best thing you can do to decrease your risk of disease and improve your health? A healthy diet of course! Consuming a diet rich in fruits and vegetables (organic is best) and healthy fats (omega 3-s and monounsaturated fats) provide your body with much-needed antioxidants to help counteract the inflammation in the body.

Try to start incorporating some of these nutrient powerhouses into your diet: salmon, flax seeds, olive oil, walnuts, avocados, berries, broccoli, kale and spinach. The healthier your diet is, the healthier your body will be. Don't compromise your health and well-being by making poor dietary choices. Choose to eat healthy, and you will help your body heal and be healthy.

"Health and fitness are totally a choice for a better quality of life."
—*Chris Powell*

CARBS — FEAR NO MORE

What's the deal with carbohydrates? Do you eat them or not? If you are trying to lose body fat, then you should not eat any carbohydrates at all, right? Wrong answer. Unfortunately, there is a lot of confusing and conflicting information out there, leaving you not knowing what to do or leading you into eating in an unhealthy manner.

So, what's the answer and what should you do?

You must view carbohydrates as an energy source. Just like gasoline is considered fuel for your car, carbohydrates are the main source of fuel for your body. If you put a small amount of gas in your car, you are not going to get far on it. It is the same with your body. If you do not eat enough carbohydrates, or in other words, give your body enough fuel, you are not going to be able to get all that far either.

Whether you are heading out to go for a run, bike ride, play tennis or go to the gym to work out — if you do not put enough fuel (carbohydrates) in your gas tank (body), you are going to run out of gas (energy).

If you are on the way to the gym to work out, and your gas gauge is on empty (as in not eating enough carbohydrates), how are you going to be able to have an effective workout?

Strength training is necessary to build and maintain muscle when trying to lose body fat. If you do not eat enough carbohydrates, your body will have to find an energy source somewhere, and unfortunately, it is from muscle. Yeah, you might be thrilled to see the scale drop a few pounds, but if it is from a loss of muscle that is not something to celebrate.

Muscle is what burns calories and what is necessary to melt that stubborn fat off.

Want to have more strength, have more energy and burn more calories? Then make sure you eat some carbs before you work out. Eating protein with your carbs is best. Doing so helps maintain blood sugar levels and helps to keep your body from burning off muscle. Eating a light meal that combines protein and carbs, 30–90 minutes prior to working out, is ideal. If you have not eaten for several hours, or say you get up to workout first thing in the morning, your internal gas gauge is on empty. You will likely feel nauseous and could possibly get sick from a quick drop in blood sugar. Not fun, and you are not going to get much of a workout in.

How are you going to get results from your workout if you do not get an effective workout in?

The best pre-workout carbs are your complex carbohydrates — like oatmeal, sweet potatoes, brown rice and whole grains. Complex carbs are broken down into simple sugars, but the sugars are released much more slowly than simple carbs. Simple carbs are your processed foods, like candy, pop and donuts. They cause your blood sugars to rise fast, which causes an increase in insulin. When this happens, it's like you're opening the door to your fat stores. Simple carbs are very easily converted to body fat and increase overall fat storage. Since complex carbs take longer to break down, they are less likely to be stored as body fat. Foods that are high in sugar, like your simple carbs, are processed by your body extremely fast.

Meaning, if they are not used for energy, they will end up on your behind quicker than you can slap it.

Amounts will vary, depending on the person and the length and intensity of the workout. A woman should eat approximately 15–25 grams of carbs with equal amounts of protein, and men should eat 30–50 grams of protein and carbs. This is just to give you estimation, since amounts for individuals can vary tremendously.

Don't fear carbs, but see them as a necessary energy source.

They are an important source of fuel needed by your body to help in your war against fat. Just like a car's gas tank, your body can only store a set amount of fuel (carbs) as well. Any excess will be stored as body fat. BUT if you put just enough gas in your car (or body) to get you where you need to go (workout), then you won't have any excess to be stored. You will be giving your body just what it needs to burn off that junk in your trunk, melt off that muffin top and power you through your workouts.

"How you start your day is how you live your day.
How you live your day is how you live your life."
Louise Hay

BREAKFAST — IT'S A BIG DEAL

Have you ever stopped to think about how the start of your day impacts the rest of your day? How many times have you found yourself running out the door in the morning skipping breakfast? Or perhaps you are not a breakfast person and just skip it all together. By now most people have heard, somehow or other, how important it is to eat a healthy breakfast, but I still find many are not heeding this advice.

What's the big deal? Does it really make that much of a difference?

You might not think it's a big deal since deciding to eat breakfast or not is just one decision.

In making the decision to eat breakfast, you are starting your day off in the right direction and setting yourself up to make healthy choices the remainder of the day.

On the flip side, when you skip out on breakfast, you are telling your body to conserve rather than burn calories. This means that your body is more likely to be in a fat-storing mode versus a fat-burning mode. Eating breakfast is like starting a fire, a fire that is your metabolism, and a fire you want to start burning and keep burning throughout the day.

Going without breakfast can also lead to low blood sugar, low energy, increased appetite and cravings later in the day.

You will be more likely to grab that donut at work, grab a fast-food meal later or make unhealthy choices. By midday you are probably starving, and by then you probably won't care how much fat or calories something has.

In addition, skipping breakfast can likely lead to justifying a bad choice later in the day. You may tell yourself, "Well I didn't have breakfast, so I can eat this hamburger and fries at lunch."

Some may think that skipping breakfast will help decrease total calorie intake for the day, and that this is a good thing. It's not. One can end up consuming too few calories, which can increase the risk of muscle loss and result in a decrease in metabolism.

So, now you have the double-whammy effect of decreased metabolism from skipping breakfast and eating too few calories. This will make it that much harder to lose weight and set the stage to gain it back easier. Your immune system will be compromised, as well as any weight loss efforts you may have.

When you eat a healthy breakfast, you are telling your body it is going to get enough calories, so all engines are a go! You fuel your body with energy and nutrients to fuel your body and mind.

You will feel better, focus better, have more energy, avoid cravings and be less likely to overeat.

In a weight loss study of breakfast eaters versus non-breakfast eaters, the group that ate breakfast as their largest meal lost the most weight. That group lost 17.8 lbs. in three months compared to 7.3 lbs. for the group that ate their largest meal at dinner.

What does a healthy breakfast consist of? Like any meal, focus on getting a balance of lean protein, complex carbohydrates or fruit, healthy fats and vegetables. My favorite: a cheese and veggie omelet with avocado and a plain baked potato with salsa. Other options are a protein smoothie, oatmeal with natural peanut butter or protein powder mixed in, or an egg sandwich on whole grain toast topped with spinach, tomato and avocado. Limited time in the morning? Prepare breakfast the night before and heat it up in the morning.

Make breakfast a part of your life, and the way you start your day.

"When you start eating food without labels, you no longer need to count calories."
—*Amanda Kraft*

CALORIE COUNTING ISN'T ENOUGH

It is believed that 80–95% of dieters gain back the majority of the weight that they fought so hard to lose. Why is that? And what can you do to help beat those odds and finally keep that weight off for good?

First of all, I think a big contributor to diet fails are a misconception that all calories are created equal. They are not. Is it always better to choose a lower-calorie food over something that is higher in calories? No. There is more to weight loss than just cutting and counting your calories. There is more to calories than meets the eye. The problem is that too many people make the mistake of not caring where their calories are coming from.

High Sugar Content

For example, let's say someone chooses to eat a 150-calorie blueberry muffin for breakfast vs. a 300-calorie peanut butter and banana protein smoothie. The muffin might seem like the better choice because it has less calories. Not the case. A muffin like this can contain 25 grams of sugar.

Sugar is very easily converted to body fat and sets the stage for your body to store even more fat.

The protein smoothie contains much less sugar, and in addition has muscle-building protein, good energizing carbohydrates and a touch of heart-healthy fat. Although higher in calories, it is a wise choice because what matters most is how your body uses those calories. The determining factor is how the food is going to affect your body. If it is mostly sugar, the sugar itself converts to body fat very easily. It not only sets the stage for your body to gain weight, but can increase cravings for sugar. Do you think that will help you lose weight? I think not.

Did you know that two people could eat the same number of calories every day for a week, and one person could lose weight and the other could gain weight?

It is all due to how your body handles the food, whether it stores it as fat or uses it for energy. What you eat is more important than just the calorie content. A lack of protein, fiber and essential nutrients can lead to weight gain even though the overall calorie content may not be that high.

Calories Too Low

If someone is overly cautious and always just choosing foods based on calorie amount, their total calorie intake for the day can easily fall too low. Not eating enough total calories can lead to a drop in metabolism and make it even harder to lose weight. It is wise to avoid high-calorie foods in general, but don't always avoid choosing a food that may offer a few more calories. If those calories are coming from protein and/or some good essential fat, it can help your weight loss efforts.

Lack of Nutrients

Let us go back to that blueberry muffin and protein smoothie. The fact that it is blueberry might trick you into thinking it is a healthy option, but it isn't very nutritious at all. It is already hard enough to get enough nutrients in your diet, so when you are trying to lose weight and eating less food overall, it makes it even harder. It is especially important to make sure your food choices are more about getting healthy nutrients versus just worrying about calories alone.

Lack of Balance

Not the standing on one foot with your eyes closed kind of balance, but a balance of nutrients. People often neglect to include protein in their meals and fear any form of fat. It is crucial to make sure that every meal has the proper balance of protein, carbohydrates, fat and fiber.

When your meals are balanced, it allows your body to burn fat for energy and is less likely to store food as fat.

Eating too many carbohydrates or foods that are high in sugar or highly processed can lead to insulin surges in your body. These insulin surges lead to sweet cravings, weight gain and a lack of energy. Getting a combination of protein, fiber and essential fats in your meals will not only help to avoid insulin surges, but will help you feel fuller longer, speed up your metabolism and allow your body to burn fat instead of creating it.

It is necessary to reduce your caloric intake in your weight loss efforts, BUT what is most important for optimal weight loss success is making the best food choices.

Better choices equal better results — a slimmer waistline and a healthier you!

"The groundwork of all happiness is good health."
—James Leigh Hunt

FEAR NOT FAT

Why would you want to include fat in your diet if that's the very thing you're trying to get rid of? You would think that eliminating all fat from your diet would be ideal, but the reality is that it's not. It's not only important to make sure you include fat in your diet, but that you get in the right kinds and the right amounts. Like with carbohydrates, in that you have your good and your bad types, you have good and bad types of fat as well. The key is to limit the bad fats and to make sure you include the good fats in your diet. Hopefully you'll learn to love what some of these wonderful fats can do for your waistline and your health.

Bad Fats

The fats you definitely want to avoid are saturated fats. Your body can actually make all that it needs. Saturated fats in your diet will more than likely end up as fat because of the high calorie amount (9 calories per gram).

In excess, these bad fats are one of your worst enemies — besides the contribution to your fat stores, they are a leading contributing factor to cardiovascular disease, some forms of cancer and insulin resistance.

Grain-fed beef and dairy products tend to have the highest amounts, so make sure to look for leaner versions if you include these foods in your diet.

Evil Fat

Trans fats are definitely the biggest enemy in our war against fat, hiding in a variety of products that you definitely want to avoid. They are often found in fried foods, bread, chips, crackers, pies, donuts, margarine and popcorn. Be sure to read your labels, as it appears as "partially hydrogenated oil" in the list of ingredients.

These fats convert to body fat easier and can cause hormonal chaos, shutting down our bodies ability to burn fat.

Trans fats have also been shown to decrease testosterone, decrease metabolism, suppress immune function, increase bad cholesterol and increase insulin. Not only bad for your belly, but bad for your body and its overall health.

Friendly Fat

Unsaturated fats are our friend and ally in the war against fat. The friendliest of these unsaturated fats are your EFAs (essential fatty acids). These fatty acids can't be synthesized by your body, so it is "essential" to include them in your diet. Not only do you need them for optimal health, but to maximize your body's ability to burn fat. A little of this friendly fat can go a long way in your weight loss efforts and with the health benefits it provides.

As long as you limit your total intake, there is no need to fear it after all.

Besides helping with weight loss, they also play an important role in hormone balancing, immune function, heart health and insulin regulation. What are some foods that contain these friendly fat fighters? Flaxseed oil, olive oil, fish, nuts and avocados.

Want to deflate that muffin top?

Be sure to include these friendly foes in your diet, as they will help you battle that stubborn belly fat.

Fear not, the fat that you fear. In other words, don't be afraid to go a little nutty sometimes, it's good for you!

"Let food by thy medicine and medicine by thy food."
—Hippocrates

EAT YOUR VEGGIES

We know we should eat them, but it is estimated that only 22% of Americans eat the suggested minimum of 3–5 servings a day. That is the suggested amount from the USDA Food Guide Pyramid, but a lot of experts suggest eating up to 1–2 pounds of vegetables a day (excluding potatoes). Regardless of the wide range of opinions that exist on the amount you should consume, the truth of the matter is that we are not eating enough.

Did you know that gorillas eat more than half of their bodyweight in vegetables alone every day? With all the huge health and weight loss benefits they have to offer, I think it's about time we start going ape over them.

Weight Loss

Low in both calories and fat, vegetables are a great guilt-free food. In addition, they help curb your appetite and cravings — they help fill you up and stay full longer. AND since it takes time for your body to break down the fiber in vegetables, it also helps to stabilize blood sugar levels.

Keeping your blood sugars stable is essential for fat loss to occur, and for the optimal health and function of your body.

Antioxidants

The protective phytonutrients (antioxidants) found in vegetables have been shown to reduce the risk of high blood pressure, diabetes, obesity and some cancers. Choosing a variety of deep leafy greens and bright colored vegetables is best, since they tend to have higher amounts of antioxidants. Variety is key, since not all vegetables are created equal. Each type will offer several health benefits of their own, but one may offer a specific nutrient only found in that particular type. For example — carrots are known to have high amounts of beta carotene which is good for eye health.

Fiber

Containing both soluble and insoluble fiber, vegetables help the digestive system and your body to reduce cholesterol and eliminate toxins. The fiber also causes you to chew your food better, lending to better digestion. Digestive issues such as bloating, gas and other forms of indigestion have been linked to inadequate chewing. As mentioned previously, Dr. Will Bulsiewicz's book, "Fiber Fueled," teaches you that you can heal your gut, improve your immune system, lose weight and improve your health dramatically — all from eating a plant-based, fiber-rich diet. These are just some of many benefits that eating "Fiber Fueled" can provide, with vegetables playing a huge part in that.

Vitamins and Minerals

Vegetables are nutrient powerhouses that offer the most nutrients per calorie. A long list of vitamins and minerals such as your B-complex vitamins, biotin, choline, and vitamins A, C, E, and K can all be found in vegetables as well as calcium and iron. It is essential to get as many nutrients from your diet as possible and not rely solely on supplements. Whole food sources of vitamins and minerals contain substances to help your body optimally absorb and utilize them. What good is a vitamin or mineral if your body cannot absorb it?

Make it a point to get these health promoting and weight management powerhouses into your diet.

No more not eating your vegetables.

It's time to quit monkeying around and do what our mothers have always told us — "Eat Your Vegetables!"

"Your diet is your bank account. Good food choices are good investments."
—Bethenny Frankel

IT STARTS WITH SHOPPING

How do you get rid of that upper arm flab? That spare tire? That jiggle when you wiggle? Do you know what one of the best exercises is to help lose body fat? Perimeter cart pushes as in grocery shopping and pushing a grocery cart around the perimeter of the store. Seriously. There is not a magic exercise that will melt off body fat from a specific area of your body.

It is not possible to selectively lose fat from your arms, abs or butt by doing isolated exercises for that given part of your bodyWhat will help you to lose that stubborn body fat is to eat properly — small frequent meals that include a balance of lean protein, complex carbohydrates and essential fats.

Diet is key to optimizing your body's ability to burn fat, so that when you do workout you can burn more body fat overall.

BUT In order to eat properly you must have the proper food available. Where can you get these essential ingredients for a fit and healthy body? At the grocery store!

Your diet is what determines your body's ability to burn fat and build muscle. Eating a diet high in calories, fat, carbs, or sugar, reduces your body's ability to burn fat and will likely keep it in a fat-storing mode.

If you want lose body fat, you need to eat in a way that will allow for your body to burn fat.

This means you need to shop for and keep stocked up on healthy essentials. Shopping the perimeter of the grocery store is where you are going to find the key "fit body" foods: the produce section for your fruits and vegetables, the meat section for lean meats and fish and the refrigerated sections for low fat cottage cheese, Greek Yogurt and eggs. I hope you are adding these items to your grocery list.

The point is, no exercise plan is going to work very well if you are not making healthy choices.

So, get out a pen and piece of paper, and let's get started on a grocery list and a trip to the store.

Some suggestions from my weekly list:

Protein: chicken, salmon, tuna (packed in water), 93% or leaner ground turkey, eggs, Greek yogurt and low-fat cottage cheese (organic and plain is best)

Complex Carbs: brown rice, oatmeal, beans, red potatoes, sweet potatoes, brown rice cakes, Kashi Go Lean cereal, steel cut oats

Fruits and vegetables: blueberries, strawberries, bananas, apples, spinach, kale, tomatoes, zucchini, squash, celery

Fats: almonds, walnuts, natural peanut butter, avocados, olive oil

Misc. snacks: Kashi TLC granola bars (for that sweet tooth and post-workout)

Remember, try to stick to the perimeter of the store as much as you can for the healthiest food choices. If you shop healthy, you can eat healthy, and in eating healthy you will shed those stubborn pounds! Happy shopping

"Happiness is the highest form of health."
—*Dalai Lama*

BEER BUSTER

I love the proverbial quote, "You can't have your cake and eat it too." It makes me think of the trade-offs and cost of the choices you make. Who doesn't want to have the best of both worlds? Who doesn't want to be able to have their cake and eat it too? The problem is we often can't have it both ways, for the trade-off and cost doesn't allow for it. In a literal sense, cake comes with a high calorie, sugar and fat content. Eating it requires a trade-off in order to fight off the negative effects it has on your health and waistline.

Like it is with cake, we want to have our beer, wine, or margarita (for example) and drink it too. It's a choice, one choice of many we are challenged with every day — from what to eat, drink or choose to do with our time and energy. So, now the question is, can one have their beer and drink it too?

Calories

When it comes to alcohol, I find that most people either don't realize, or don't care to know (but should), the calorie and sugar content of their drinks. As with food, it comes down to making good choices and an awareness of what you consume. With beer, choosing a lower-calorie option is typically best (choosing light over regular), but it's not always the case. It's about the total calories consumed. For example, if you like to drink a high-calorie beer, but you drink less of them than you typically would with a light beer, it would be your best choice as you would be drinking fewer overall calories. Dry red wine is the best choice with wine, with less sugar than sweeter wines and more antioxidants than white wines. With mixed drinks, opt for low-calorie and low-sugar mixers, and avoid frozen drinks (high sugar content).

With the popular emergence of all the "low carb" beers, people often forget that it's still calories.

A bigger mistake is that they rarely ever realize that alcohol has more calories than carbs. Carbs have 4 calories per gram and alcohol has 7 calories per gram. In reality, alcohol is like a concentrated carb. It's almost as high in calories as fat, which has 9 calories per gram.

First of all, we need to realize that alcohol is an energy source for our body. If you were to drink 3 light beers at 100 calories each, that would equal 300 calories. For someone that's on a diet plan consisting of 5 meals of 300 calories, those 3 beers equal the number of calories of 1 entire meal. Even if you were to stick to your diet *to a T*, those 3 beers would be an extra 300 calories added to your calorie intake for the day.

If you're trying to lose weight, the alcohol calories can easily creep up and keep you from being in the negative calorie balance that you want and need to lose weight.

Timing

The trick is to not only be smart about what you're drinking, but about what and when you're eating as well. If you know you're going to go out for drinks in the evening, then plan for it calorie-wise, and try to eat a little lighter that day. Try to eat less carbs and fat prior to your night out so you have some wiggle room with your calories. Don't skip any meals during the day and ideally eat a light meal with lean protein and vegetables before having drinks. It will help keep up your metabolism, keep your blood sugar stable and help reduce cravings and the urge to overeat. Try not to drink with meals, or keep it to a minimum, since the calories you get from alcohol can add up to a meal's worth in no time.

Keep in mind, that your body uses the calories from alcohol before it uses any from food.

Any excess will most likely get stored as body fat. The more one drinks, the more one typically eats, and the more likely they'll eat late at night as well. The likelihood that someone will make healthy food choices decreases the more one drinks. A few drinks aren't so bad calorie-wise, but stopping at a drive-thru for a hamburger and fries is (even worse if you do this right before going to sleep).

Know Effects

Drinking as little as possible is ideal since higher levels of alcohol will affect your brain's ability to make good decisions. More than that though, it's knowing alcohol's huge affect on your hormones.

Drinking alcohol can lower blood sugar, increase estrogen levels, slow metabolism and increase fat storage.

It pretty much shuts down your body's ability to burn fat for several hours. Those effects, added to one's typical poor dietary choices after a few cocktails, is what causes beer bellies, inflated love handles and jiggly thighs. If you're careful about what you eat and drink, and don't make a habit of drinking too much or often, you shouldn't have too much to worry about if you want to go have a drink. It's up to you what you do. You tell me, can you have your beer and drink it too?

"Just because you aren't making progress as fast as you think you should does not mean you aren't making progress. Keep going."
—*Unknown*

COMMON CULPRITS

Do you ever feel that you are doing all the right things, eating better, even exercising, and just not making the progress you feel you should be? It's often two common culprits causing the problem. Can you guess what they are? Undereating and overexercising.

Even though you would expect to lose weight from eating healthier and exercising, if you are not eating enough calories it can impede your progress.

In some cases, people may need to eat more calories and exercise less. I know it can seem hard to believe, but I've had quite a few clients where this was the case. How is that possible? Let's take a closer look at the calorie needs of our body.

Your body needs a set number of calories a day just to do its daily functions, such as maintaining body temperature, breathing, circulation, digestion and cellular processes. If you were laying on the couch and did absolutely nothing all day, your body would still require a set number of calories to perform its functions. This is called BMR, which stands for Basal Metabolic Rate. I like to refer to it as one's "base metabolism." BMR calculations are based on sex, age, weight and body composition. Men will typically have a higher BMR than women because of differing body composition, as men typically have more muscle mass.

Your BMR is a calculated estimate of the number of calories your body needs to do its daily functions. The calories needed for your body to get through a typical day is called daily energy expenditure. This calculation includes exercise and daily activities like shopping, walking to the car, cleaning and chasing after your kids. The more kids you have, and the faster they are, will definitely increase that amount.

This daily expenditure is averaged out over a week to give you an amount that equals your maintenance level of calories. This is an estimate of

the calories you would need to take in on a daily basis. If you were to eat your maintenance level of calories, you would be, in essence, giving your body the precise amount of energy (calories) to get through each day. When you eat this "maintenance" amount, you shouldn't gain or lose weight, but "maintain" your weight.

I'll use myself for an example.

BMR = 1394 calories
Maintenance Level = 2200 calories

In order for me to lose weight, I would need to eat less than my maintenance level of calories, but not below my BMR.

What I often see is that people trying to lose weight usually cut their calories too low. Eating a calorie amount below your BMR can eventually cause your metabolism to slow down AND your body to burn muscle in order to supply its energy needs. Muscle is a precious commodity that you don't want to lose. Muscle is what you need to burn off the fat. The more muscle one has, the more calories their body can burn every day, even at rest.

Even if you're exercising, your metabolism can slow down if you're not eating enough calories.

If you aren't eating enough to give your body its minimum functional requirements (BMR), you create an even bigger deficit by adding in exercise. Your body's metabolism will eventually slow down because now it is running low on fuel. It needs to perform its daily functions and fuel a workout. It's like having a muscle car with an 8-cylinder engine and you're giving it only a few gallons of gas to get through the day. To become more efficient, your body will adjust by operating like a 4-cylinder car so it can function on less gas.

You want a calorie deficit to lose weight, but you don't want to wreak havoc on your metabolism.

You want to exercise to help burn calories, but you need proper rest and an adequate amount of calories and nutrients to help you recover. To get a quick idea of what your exact calorie needs are, you can find online calculators or you can get a body composition test to more accurately determine your calorie needs.

It's best to strive for 1–2 lbs. of weight loss a week. The 3500-calorie deficit rule to lose 1 lb. of fat is outdated. It's not a bad estimate to use for a rough idea, but there are better tools to more accurately estimate calorie needs. Unfortunately, it predicts slower progress than what people are used to, but with it one can set more realistic goals and know what to expect.

Experts at the NIH (National Institute of Heath) created a new complex formula — "The Body Weight Simulator" — a weight planner for assessing weight loss trajectory. Multiple mathematical calculations are involved in this weight loss predictor. The calculations take into account weight, height, age, activity level, goal weight and length of time to reach goal weight. It provides a calorie level for both weight loss and maintenance. This formula is in the process of being patented and is thought to be the way of the future.

The best way to lose weight is to combine strength training, cardiovascular training and a balanced nutrition plan.

The key is to make sure you don't drop your calories too low. You have to account for exercise needs if you're dieting and trying to lose weight. You can't work out like a horse and eat like a rabbit. You need to give your body what it needs to maximize your metabolism, have effective workouts, and burn fat versus slowing its metabolism and conserving it. AND no, it's not a reason to add a donut a day to your diet, but you may need to eat a little more than you think.

"Slow progress is still progress."
—Megan Auman

SLOW AND STEADY WINS THE RACE

As a child, I remember how much I loved the story "The Tortoise and the Hare" from Aesop's Fables. It really stuck with me, and it later became useful in my line of work. The concept of "slow and steady wins the race" was one I used often when working with clients to explain the science of weight loss. When it comes to weight loss, who doesn't want to lose weight fast? As established in the previous chapter, it's vitally important that you eat an adequate number of calories on a daily basis. But what often happens, is that people want to lose weight faster, so they cut calories. Sometimes knowingly, sometimes not.

One can easily fall victim to false information.

There are a number of mobile apps and online tools that people often use to track their food intake. Used as a tool to track your food intake, they're great. BUT it's critical to know an important thing about the ability of the majority of these food trackers to accurately calculate your calorie needs: they often FAIL to provide you with an appropriate number of calories to meet YOUR specific calorie needs.

The information is often false and inaccurate, which can cause one to be eating far fewer calories than what would be ideal and optimal for weight loss.

For example, most fitness trackers have you input your age, weight and height. Then they will ask you how much weight you want to lose per week and the time frame you would like to reach your goal by. Most people input that they would like to lose the maximum 2 lbs. per week. Who wouldn't? The problem with this is that it almost always calculates a calorie level that is too low, often falling below someone's BMR. In the short term, one can lose weight, but it will likely lead to slowing down their metabolism.

It can lead to loss of muscle, fatigue, cravings, increases in hunger and your body slamming the brakes on weight loss.

Fitness trackers also overestimate how much you can lose over a long period of time. For tracking food intake, they're an awesome tool. As a calculator for weight loss, they are not.

I'll use myself as an example. I input my age, height and weight, and set a goal to lose 2 lbs. per week. I input that I would like to lose 15 lbs. in 2 months' time.

Under "activity level," if I input the following, these are the daily calorie amounts it suggests for me:

Inactive = 594 calories
Somewhat active = 926 calories
Extremely active = 1391 calories

My BMR is 1394, which is my calorie needs with zero activity. If I was extremely active, I would have a maintenance level of calories in the 2000s. If I was to only eat 1394 calories as this suggests, I would be starving my body of its energy needs. I would be giving my body what it needs at rest, not in an extremely active state.

If I considered myself to be inactive, I would starve at a 594-calorie intake. A lot of people that use these apps are inactive, and this is the number of calories that would be suggested for them. This example demonstrates the unfortunate flaw in their calculating system that can really lead people astray.

If you are going to use these apps and online tools, when it comes to setting a weight loss goal, input that you would like to lose 1 lb. per week. I find that this usually will more accurately estimate your calorie needs to a safer, more sustainable and effective weight loss amount. I can't guarantee that this will be an appropriate amount though. Do yourself a favor and look up online BMR calculators. If you eat a little over your BMR, say 100–200 calories, that will be a much safer calorie level to eat for safe, long-term weight loss.

As much as we all would like to hop, hop, hop as fast as possible to our goal weight finish line, we have to remember, it's slow and steady that wins the race.

3

THE EXERCISE PILLAR

"To enjoy the glow of health, you must exercise."
—*Gene Tunny*

EXERCISE — IT'S JUST AMAZING!

Believe it or not, I would still exercise even if I knew I couldn't lose weight from it. I just feel so much better mentally and psychically when I do it; I would never want to go without it. The benefits from exercise alone are greatly beneficial, and in conjuction with diet, are life altering, life saving and life enhancing.

BUT just as we should not only have one pillar, as in only dieting (the Diet Pillar), we should not rely solely on exercise (the Exercise Pillar). We need both: a sound diet plan (the Diet Pillar) and an effective exercise plan (the Exercise Pillar) to optimize our health and weight loss efforts.

Exercise has immensely positive effects on both our mental and physical health.

Exercise improves overall health, improves sleep, reduces symptoms of depression, strengthens our immune system and helps to release negative emotions in a positive way. The positive effects of exercise combat just about every negative effect of stress, and the stressreducing benefits can be a life saver.

Whether it is weight training, walking, running, swimming or yoga — they all are great in their own way. They are all extremely helpful in reducing stress and keeping your mind and body young.

Did you know that doing balance exercises, such as those done in yoga, help to increase brain function and slow the aging process?

It is pretty amazing. A little exercise can go a long way, and any amount is better than doing nothing. Something will help, doing nothing won't. So, let's dive in to learning some amazing ways exercise can help you on your path to optimal health and wellness.

"Health is like money; we never have a true idea of its value
until we lose it."
—Josh Billings

HEALTH IS WEALTH

What's your favorite thing about the new year? For me, it's the feeling of a new beginning, like a fresh slate and a mountain of motivation to achieve my goals.

Unfortunately, I find that most people get focused solely on losing weight and not on what's most important, your health. Although being at your ideal weight is important, those other numbers — your blood pressure, cholesterol and blood sugar — all need to be at healthy levels too.

Exercise should be about being fit and healthy, not just weight loss.

Why? I'm happy to explain.

What is the leading cause of death for both men and women? Heart disease. Yet, people are still overweight, smoke, are physically inactive and have horrible diets. All these are risk factors for getting heart disease, and risk factors that that can be controlled. Your heart works harder than any muscle in the body and is the most important one we need to take care of. If you have an average heart rate of 80 beats per minute, it will beat 4,800 beats an hour, and 115,200 a day. If you live to be 80 years old, your heart would have beaten 3,363,840,000 times!

Don't make your heart work any harder than it has to by being overweight, smoking, having high blood pressure or making poor diet choices.

Being overweight puts strain on your heart and increases your chances of heart disease. Smoking increases heart rate, blood pressure and the tendency for blood to clot — increasing your risk two to four times. The chemicals found in cigarettes also harden blood cells and can damage the function of the heart and blood vessels. High blood pressure causes the heart to thicken and become stiffer, just as high cholesterol does to your arteries. Having high blood sugar can increase cholesterol and damage your arteries as well.

Let's say at the age of 40, you decide to get your heart in better shape and lower your resting heart rate 10 beats per minute. That 10 beats a minute less will save you 210,240,000 beats by the time you turn 80. That's 5 years!

Don't wait until you have a serious health issue before you decide to take action for your health.

Not everyone will be lucky enough to survive a heart attack.

Just as one wouldn't view eating and sleeping as optional, we need to view exercise in the same manner. We need to be serious about our health and build it into our daily lives. Think about all the choices you make when it comes to the health of their body. The time is now to start making good choices with your diet, lifestyle and life.

Exercise and a heart-healthy diet are proven to help decrease the risk of heart disease.

Control your risk factors and control your health. Power is prevention. It's not the weight you lose, but the life you gain!

"It's never too late to take your heart health seriously and make it a priority."
—Jennie Garth

CREATING A HEALTHY AND HAPPY HEART

What would you consider the most important muscle to keep strong in your body? I bet that not many people would answer "heart" or even think of the heart as a muscle. Cardiovascular exercise is necessary to keep the heart muscle strong, for it's the heart that pumps blood throughout the body — to vital organs and muscles in our body, delivering oxygen and nutrients needed for optimal performance and energy. If your heart is weak, it will have to work harder (faster heart rate) compared to if it was fitter (slower heart rate).

Like mileage on a car, you're only good for so many miles. A person that is out of shape will have a higher heart rate than someone that is more in shape and cardiovascularly fit. This leads to them acquiring higher mileage on their heart much quicker than a person that is in shape and has a lower-than-average heart rate.

Make sense? A person that does regular, consistent bouts of cardiovascular exercise strengthens their heart muscle, and when your heart becomes stronger, your resting heart rate lowers. A strong heart means your heart can pump more blood every time it contracts, therefore it doesn't have to contract as often.

With a stronger heart, you will get more mileage out of it, so to speak.

Also, by being stronger, your heart can deliver more nutrients and oxygen throughout your body. Regarding fitness, this means more nutrients and oxygen to your muscles, which leads to increases in muscular strength, endurance and an increased capacity to build more muscle mass.

Not only will it help you to have more energy, but help your body to become a lean, mean, fat-fighting machine.

How? Besides just burning calories, aerobic exercise increases your body's ability to burn fat. It does this by increasing the fat burning enzymes in your muscles.

Simply speaking, it helps your body to become more efficient at burning fat versus storing it.

How much?

The recommended amounts: 150 minutes of moderate activity (brisk walking) or 75 minutes of vigorous activity (jogging or running). You can increase the frequency and duration depending on your goals and fitness levels. Unless you're training for a race or specific endurance event, cardio shouldn't exceed the 30-minute mark. You're better off doing 2 x 30-minute sessions vs. one long hour session.

This is due to the law of diminishing returns, meaning the amount of fat your body burns decreases with an increase in the length of cardio.

So, either exercise at a higher intensity for a shorter amount of time, or split up your cardio sessions to get the most out of your time and effort.

Intensity

A way to measure your intensity with cardio is by utilizing heart rate training. You can use the heart rate handles on a cardio machine, a heart rate watch or by just simply taking your pulse (take for 10 seconds and multiply x 6). There are typically heart rate charts hanging up at gyms and posted on cardio equipment.

When doing cardio, you want your exercising heart rate to be at a level where your heart is beating fast enough to be in the "fat burning" zone, but not so fast to where it's a strain on your heart and you can't keep up the pace. Endurance athletes can train at higher intensities, but the *average Joe* should be careful not to get their heart rates too high.

You want to be exercising hard enough to where you're breathing harder, as in needing more oxygen, but not so hard as to where you are out of breath.

You can tell this by doing the talk test — you should be able to talk during exercise and need to take a breath every few words, but not so out of breath where you can't talk at all.

If you use the heart rate method and take your pulse, and there are no heart rate charts, then use the following method.

To calculate the "fat burning zone," you would take 60–70% of your maximum heart rate. Maximum heart rate is calculated by subtracting your age from 220.

For example, let's use a 50-year-old.

*Note — this method is for estimation only and is one of the simplest to use; other methods can be utilized as well.

220 - 50 (age) = 170 (maximum heart rate) .... for safety and training reasons, you don't want your heart rate to exceed 85% of this rate = 144.5 (or 145)

"Fat Burning Zone"

170 (maximum heart rate) x 60% = 102

170 (maximum heart rate) x 70% = 119

So, for a 50-year-old, the "fat burning zone" would be 102–119. If you walk slowly on a treadmill, you may need to speed it up a little to make sure you get your heart rate up high enough to where it's more effective. For you treadmill walkers — don't hold on to the railings of a treadmill, pump your arms to get that heart rate up and burn more calories. If that doesn't do the trick, then hit the incline to increase the intensity and heart rate a bit.

Before or After Strength Training?

Cardio can be done before strength training as a method of warming up your muscles, but shouldn't be longer than 5–10 minutes. To get the most out of your workouts, meaning optimal fat burning and overall strength and endurance, doing cardio AFTER you lift weights is best.

Why?

You want to burn fat during cardio and be your strongest when you lift weights. This will equate to good overall muscle strength and endurance.

Let's say you run for 30 minutes on a treadmill, then lift weights afterwards.

Doing cardio beforehand burns off a lot of your body's glycogen, which is the stored form of carbohydrates in your muscles. Glycogen is the energy source you want and need for strength training, for without it you run out of gas — you won't be able to lift as much weight and will fatigue quicker.

If you weight train first, you will have a much higher supply of this precious muscle glycogen, which you want. Being able to lift more weight and get more total reps will help equate to more muscle being built, more calories being burned and more fat being lost.

Who wouldn't want that? Also, weight training will end up burning off a lot of your body's glycogen supply (which you want), so when you go to do cardio after you lift you will be able to access and burn off your body fat stores easier and quicker. Again, who doesn't want that?

You don't have to go to a gym to do cardio — you can walk, swim, bike ride, dance, etc. Anything that gets your heart rate up for a continued amount of time is considered cardio. You can get a good cardiovascular workout without even moving out of a stationary spot. For example, you can walk in place, do jumping jacks, jump rope, etc. Any form of cardiovascular exercise is beneficial, the important thing is that you do it, and do it long enough and on a consistent basis.

You can't afford to skip out on the benefits aerobic exercise can provide you.

Aerobic activity enhances emotional positivity, helping you to feel happier, feel better and feel less stressed. AND with it you get more "life miles," and with that a healthier and stronger heart. A strong heart is a fit heart, and with a fit heart comes a healthier and happier you!

"Those who do not find time to exercise will have to find time for illness."
—Edward Smith-Stanley

COUCH POTATOES BEWARE

As if there weren't already enough couch potatoes, the stay-at-home orders from the coronavirus pandemic might have created quite a few more. I'm aware that I've had a bit more couch time than usual, and I've noticed a few more pounds creeping up again. Hello muffin top. Say goodbye to your belly, your muffin top and to the couch. We must get off the couch and get moving!

America, it's time to take a stand against the new health risks a lot of us are unknowingly facing — prolonged sitting and inactivity. Whether its commute time, time spent on the computer, at work, or sitting on the couch watching television, Americans are spending more time being inactive than ever before.

Sadly, it's been estimated that 30% of Americans are considered inactive (sedentary), with studies reporting averages ranging from 2000–4400 steps per day.

Not only that, an average of eight to nine hours a day are spent sitting.

An active lifestyle is 10,000 steps or more, and an inactive lifestyle is less than 5,000 steps a day. And Americans are nowhere near to getting the recommended 10,000 steps a day, which equates to exercising strenuously for thirty minutes or walking five miles (approximate value).

Prolonged sedentary behavior is dangerous to our health. It is linked to diabetes, obesity, high blood pressure, high cholesterol, heart disease, chronic inflammation and increased risk of death. Studies have shown that people whose days involved long stretches of sitting for thirty minutes or more, had the highest risk if total sitting time also exceeded 12.5 hours a day.

In a National Institute of Health study, those who sat more than thirteen hours per day had twice the risk of death compared to those who sat less than eleven hours.

Those who sat less than thirty minutes a day, had 55% lower risk, compared to those that sat longer than thirty minutes at a time. And those that sat more than ninety minutes a day had two times the risk than those that always sat less than ninety minutes. Some theorize that this is due to reduced insulin sensitivity and less calorie expenditure.

Prolonged inactivity has been shown to cause reductions in glucose uptake, negatively impacting cholesterol levels — increasing the LDL (bad cholesterol) and decreasing the HDL (good cholesterol).

Think you don't have to worry about this it because you exercise? Think again.

Even though one may exercise, this inactivity can still cause harm and increase health risks. It is known as the "active couch potato phenomenon."

Increases in one's total sitting time increased risk of early death, despite age, sex, race, BMI or exercise habits. This doesn't mean that exercise isn't beneficial or that it doesn't help offset this. One would be at much higher risk if they did not exercise at all. It's more about the fact that long durations of inactivity are detrimental to one's health despite the fact they exercise.

For example, take someone that walks for thirty minutes a day but sits for ten hours a day. The harm from being sedentary for that length of time is exponentially higher than the benefit from the time spent walking.

Does one have to move around all day to avoid their own demise? Not at all. Just stand up. Move a little. Walk down the hall at work to get a quick drink of water.

A little will go a long way in helping to break up typical long periods of inactivity and offset the effects of prolonged sitting.

It is believed that just the act of standing helps to engage muscles and negate the impending harm from sitting too long.

The key is to try to create more activity versus reducing it. It's nice to sit down and relax, but don't just opt to do so out of habit. Choose to stand versus always taking a seat. Go to the bathroom upstairs at work, skip the elevator and walk on your breaks. Stop circling parking lots at the store or work to find a closer spot; park farther away on purpose.

Break the habit of sitting on the couch every night, and take a leisurely stroll or casual bike ride instead.

Break up periods of TV watching with short breaks of walking in place or stretching. Wear a Fitbit or pedometer, or use a fitness app on your phone — to not only get an awareness of how active you truly are, but to challenge yourself to move more.

Take steps today, and every day, for better health and to be a fitter, better you!

"Health is the greatest gift of human blessings."
—Hippocrates

BRAIN HEALTH

Just In case you needed another reason as to why you should exercise, here's another one that should go to the top of the list: regular aerobic exercise can help improve memory and thinking skills. We often just associate doing cardiovascular exercise with the heart, but it's just as important for our brain health.

Being that one in ten people in the United States 65 and older has Alzheimer's dementia (the most common form of dementia), it's something that needs to be brought to our attention. During the fourteen-year time period between 2000–2014, Alzheimer's-related deaths increased an alarming 89%.

Our bodies are under attack from the consumption of processed foods, sugar, corn syrup, lack of exercise and stress.

These factors cause oxidative stress in the body, which leads to inflammation and atherosclerosis of the blood vessels (like rusty pipes). This causes the vital organs of the body — the brain and heart — to not get the necessary oxygen and nutrients they need to function properly. The scary result of this can lead to a heart attack, stroke or death.

The known culprits to heart disease are the same culprits that affect our brain health.

The buildup of plaque in the arteries and the stiffening of arteries one gets with age, can not only reduce the supply of oxygen to the heart, but to the brain as well. This reduced blood flow damages the heart and also puts your brain at risk of being damaged.

A stroke, which is often referred to as a "brain attack," is like a heart attack of the brain. High blood pressure is often found to be the leading cause of this. If you're lucky enough to survive one, chances are that you will likely develop dementia (one out of every three survivors do).

There are an estimated five million Americans living with Alzheimer's disease, and one in three seniors die from Alzheimer's or other dementias. It's not just a disease, it's an epidemic. We all experience some cognitive decline with age, which typically begins at age 45.

What we don't want to experience is a faster decline, or a faster loss of memory or brain function.

One common thing I found among all the research articles I've read, is the affect of exercise on the brain. A University of Pittsburgh study compared a group of seniors that walked 40 minutes, three times a week, at a moderate pace, to other groups that did stretching, yoga and exercise with resistance bands. The walking group amazingly showed an increase in the hippocampus, the part of their brain responsible for short-term memory. This part of the brain typically shrinks as we age and is not known to get bigger. Furthermore, this is the part of the brain that Alzheimer's affects greatly.

Another University of Pittsburgh study on 78-year-olds showed that the seniors that walked six to nine miles a week had more gray matter (volume) in their brain than their less active peers. The researchers tested them nine years later, and found that the active group cut their risk of cognitive impairment and dementia by 50%. Pretty amazing. I think I'll go out for another walk!

What can you do to protect your heart and brain? Eat healthier, put down that cigarette, start exercising and take care of yourself.

Think of your body like a high-performance car — we would never use dirty fuel or put sugar in our gas tank and expect high performance.

How do you give your brain that high-octane fuel it so desires and needs? Eat a healthy diet with organic produce, nuts, beans, fiber and healthy fats. Want to keep both your heart and brain healthy? Fuel your body with premium unleaded and get your wheels rolling to a healthier and happier heart, mind and body!

"The secret of getting ahead is getting started."
—*Mark Twain*

ACTION CREATES MOTIVATION

Too tired to exercise? How are you going to get any energy if you don't start moving? Most people are tired because they are not getting in any exercise. The best way to motivate is to act. Action creates motivation. You are not going to get motivated sitting on the couch, watching TV. If you have time to sit and watch TV, you have time to exercise.

We just can't sit around and expect to get energy *out of the blue*. Exercise will increase your energy levels, help you sleep betterand improve your health in numerous ways.

You don't need to go from zero to sixty, or run a marathon on your first day, you just need to start moving.

Actions can be as simple as going for a walk every day on your lunch break. Even if it's just walking to the end of the block, the end of your driveway, it's something.

Need help in the motivation department? Make a list of songs to help motivate you into action. Music is my savior and is something I depend on to help spark my motivation to workout. Listening to music helps to not only motivate me to work out, it helps me to have a much better and enjoyable workout as well.

It's time to get moving — to get off your rock and get it rolling!

Mind Over Muffin Top Activity

What are ways you can increase your activity?

What reminders can you put in place to help?

How will you track your activity?

*"It is a shame for a man to grow old without seeing
the beauty and strength of which his body is capable."*
—*Socrates*

STRENGTH TRAINING

No matter what age you start, regular muscle-strengthening exercises can slow, even reverse, the deterioration of muscle mass. Strength training is an essential part of a fitness program but becomes increasingly important the older one gets. Cardiovascular exercise such as walking, jogging or swimming is very important and needed as well, but it's not enough.

We need strength training — a minimum of 2–3 times a week to increase strength, muscle mass and bone density.

Why? According to research, as we age, we tend to gain weight — 1 to 2 lbs. a year. The average weight gain for women from 45–55 yrs. of age is 12–15 lbs. (thanks menopause). And after the age of 30, muscle loss averages 3–8% per decade. It's also estimated that post-menopausal women lose 1–2% of their bone mass every year.

This is because a female's production of estrogen drastically declines after menopause. Estrogen prevents the breakdown of bone and helps keep them strong. The best way to counteract that is by doing muscle-strengthening exercises — not only does it strengthen your muscles, it strengthens your bones. In addition, your balance and coordination improve, and you decease your chance of falls and injuries. One bad fall, a broken hip, and your life is changed forever.

The sad thing is a lot of us just think that because we're getting older, there is no hope. It doesn't have to be an inevitable part of aging, and you can keep from being a part of those depressing statistics.

You can fight it — you can be a fitter, stronger, slimmer and "younger" you — all from strength training!

Lifting weights helps to increase your fat burning machinery. What's that fat burning machinery? Muscle. By adding just 1 lb. of muscle, your body will be able to burn an extra 50 calories a day, even at rest. When trying to lose weight, you want to ensure that you build and/or maintain as much of this precious commodity as possible. Building, or at least maintaining your lean body mass (muscle), will help keep your metabolism up and keep the pounds off.

Did you know that you can burn more calories from weightlifting than you can from doing cardio? What's the reason?

Strength training has a greater "after burn" than cardio.

Even though someone can burn more calories in the time period of a workout (for example, a 30-minute workout), someone that does a strength training workout can burn more calories over the course of the day than a person that did cardio only.

Let's say I do a 30-minute, total body strength training workout, and a friend of mine does a 30-minute jogging session on a treadmill. In that 30-minute time frame, say my friend burns 200 calories, and I burn 150 calories. BUT, over the course of several hours, I burn a total of 300 calories, and my friend, 250 calories. I end up burning more calories overall.

How is this possible? I describe it like this — if you drive a car hard and fast, the engine really heats up, and it takes longer to cool off the hotter it is. This is what strength training is like. And the more muscle you have, the bigger your engine (muscle) is, and the more gas (calories) it's going to burn off. Jogging on a treadmill will warm up the engine, but not to the degree of heat that strength training does. This is because strength training is typically a more intense workout.

If you're not familiar with how to properly do strength training, you can hire a trainer, attend a workshop, or class. You want to make sure you do strength training exercises correctly, to avoid injury and get optimal benefits. For those that prefer to avoid gyms, there are plenty of things you can do at home. Balance balls, resistance bands and dumbbells are available at any sporting goods store or you can order online.

You can also rent or purchase DVDs or access programs and videos on the internet. If that doesn't interest you, try water aerobics classes. Exercising in the water is great way to strengthen muscles without the worry of putting stress on your joints. The point is, like my favorite ad slogan by Nike says, "Just Do It!" You just have to do it, pick up that dumbbell and lift your way to a fitter, stronger and slimmer you!

*"The hardest lift of all, is lifting your butt
off the couch." —unknown*

"Efficiency is doing things right; effectiveness is doing the right things."
—*Peter Drucker*

FIX YOUR FORM

What is the biggest and most common mistake I see people make with their workout routines? Improper exercise form. Every gym I've ever been in could hire someone full-time just to go around from person-to-person, instructing them on correct exercise techniques. I think you have a combination of people that think they are doing things correctly, but are not, and some that really just don't know what to do but try anyway. Whatever the case may be, doing exercises improperly is the grand-daddy of all no-nos.

Start Small

Unlike the saying, "Go big or go home," when it comes to starting out on a fitness journey, it's more of a "go small or go home" ideal. When I say start small, I am referring to (and highly stress) the importance of starting out in a small class, or working one-on-one with a qualified personal trainer.

Why? When someone joins a gym or participates in a group exercise class, they often go about doing things without proper instruction or guidance. Take a large group class for example — there are often too many people for the instructor to be able to correct everyone's exercise form. This could lead to an injury and negatively affect the quality of your workout.

This holds especially true for beginners, as one should not only be shown proper form, but modifications to better accommodate their level of fitness.

Exercise and yoga videos are great tools to use, but there still isn't a trained eye to watch your form and determine if you're doing the exercises correctly. You may also need to modify exercises or avoid certain ones if you have had any injuries or have any limitations.

Only after you have learned how to exercise with proper form should you ever start working out in a gym or attend a large-size class. You want to do things the right way and the best way to help you achieve your goals.

Getting sessions with a personal trainer or taking small group classes is the best decision you can make to help start you out on the right track with your health and fitness goals.

Risk of Injury

Doing exercises too fast or with improper form can lead to muscle strains and muscle tears. In general, exercise machines are safer to use than free weights, but they can still be used terribly wrong. If it's not set up properly, or if you don't use them correctly, you increase the chances of hurting yourself even more. For example — the pec fly machine. If the range of motion pins are set too far back, someone could easily suffer a serious shoulder tear.

Muscle Development

To get the maximum benefit out of an exercise, a muscle should be used in its full range of motion. For example, a dumbbell bicep curl. Your elbows should be "glued" to your sides when performing this exercise, and the weight lowered just short of the arm being totally straight (slight bend in elbow when extended).

What commonly happens is that people often only lower the weight halfway down and tend to raise their elbows when the weight is lifted. Doing this "incorrect" movement actually works more of the shoulder muscle than the biceps. This can lead to overtraining the shoulder muscle and result in very little muscle or strength gains in the muscle you're actually trying to work.

Learn

It's best to ask for help if needed, so you can learn how to do exercises correctly and safely. Books and exercise magazines can be valuable and helpful resources to help learn how to do exercises properly. Be aware though, because a lot of times a few key points to an exercise's form might not be stated.

You may think you understand how to do an exercise, and think you are doing it correctly, but actually NOT.

Sometimes people are even shown how to use machines properly, whether through a gym orientation or a session with a personal trainer. BUT when they go to work out on their own, they either forget how to do everything correctly or never learned how to do them properly in the first place. It takes practice and feedback — practice doing the exercise correctly, with feedback on key points to help you remember how to do the exercises correctly.

Mirrors

Did you know that mirrors in the gym are actually there for visual feedback, rather than for people to admire themselves while working out? Using the mirrors allows you to visualize yourself performing the exercise, to use as a visual feedback tool to make adjustments to your form.

Proper exercise form is extremely important but commonly abused. Don't risk hurting yourself, or waste your time and efforts by doing exercises incorrectly. It takes more than knowing how to do something, it takes doing it.

*"Give me 6 hours to chop down a tree and I will spend the
first four hours sharpening the axe."*
—Abraham Lincoln

THE POWER OF PLANNING

If you were given an axe and told to go cut a tree down, chances are almost every single one of us would just start chopping right off the bat. You would likely think that the sooner you get moving, the quicker you will complete your task and cut down that tree. If Abraham Lincoln were still around, that wouldn't be the case. His quote above shows how brilliant he truly was.

Quite typically when it comes to achieving a goal, we want to do it quickly and start moving right away. This type of action and thinking usually ends up extending the time to achieving your goals or not achieving them at all. You are not going to be able to cut down a tree very well with a dull axe. Abe Lincoln's quote shows just how important it is to plan and the significance of preparation. Many goals fail due to a lack of both.

Without a plan, precious time and energy is often wasted, leading to frustration and increased difficulty in achieving your goals.

If you are trying to lose weight and get in shape, wouldn't you rather work smarter, not harder? Why put in more effort and extend the time it takes to achieve your goals than you need to? Unfortunately, I see so many people make this mistake in the gym and with their diets, doing things incorrectly and not really knowing what to do. It is hard enough to get motivated to work out and make diet changes without wasted time and energy from doing things incorrectly or inefficiently.

With the proper tools and knowledge, like having a sharper axe, you can chop away at the extra weight you're carrying and carve out a fit and healthy body.

What is one of the most important tools you can sharpen? Your mind. Increase your knowledge, and seek out the advice and help from experts if needed.

Make your "axe" even sharper by fueling your body and mind with a healthy, balanced diet and proper sleep. You wouldn't blindly start chopping away at a tree with a dull axe. You don't want to blindly chop away at your health and fitness goals with a dull axe either. Sharpen that axe, take the time to prepare and plan, and you'll cut down the trees (and blocks) that are standing in front of you and your goals.

"Success is the sum of small efforts repeated day-in and day-out."
—*Robert Collier*

STARTING ON THE RIGHT FOOT

Whether you've been working out for years or a newcomer to exercise, you want to get the most out of your time and efforts. If you don't really know what you're doing when it comes to diet or exercise, don't you think it would be a good idea to start off on the right foot and the right track from the beginning? I've found that many people think they are doing things properly, but the reality is they're not. The sad truth is that it's usually far from what is ideal for optimal weight loss and strength gains. From what I've seen and experienced personally, I would say at least 80% of the people I see working out in a gym could benefit from a few changes (or a lot of changes) to their diet and/or workout routines.

Most people get into a routine with their diet and exercise regimen — they keep doing the same thing but want and expect a different result.

It doesn't make much sense, but chances are you could be guilty of it yourself. If I told you to CHANGE everything you're currently doing, and to totally revamp your exercise and diet routine, would you do it? Did you feel any resistance to that question? It's OK, more than likely you did, it's our nature. We get comfortable doing what's familiar, and we develop habits and routines that are hard to break. So, what's my point?

Get Help

There's nothing I hate more than to see people putting in serious time and energy into their workout, but not getting the results they want. When it comes to someone's diet, I find that people get stuck at frustrating weight-loss plateaus as well.

You may "think" you're eating healthy, but are you eating in an optimal way to maximize muscle gain and burn body fat?

You may be exercising, but are you doing the exercises correctly? Do you know what you're doing when you work out? Do you have a result-driven exercise routine, or do you just do what you "think" works? Don't be afraid to ask for help. Consulting with a nutritionist and/or a personal trainer could be one of the best investments you ever make in yourself. Doing so can help give you the necessary tools and knowledge to achieve the results you want. As with anything, go with known references. When it comes to seeking help of any kind, the experience, knowledge, level of expertiseand personality can vary greatly. Choose wisely, make it be a fit for you and in turn help you to be fit!

"The best advice I ever got was that knowledge is power and to keep reading."
—David Bailey

HEEDING ADVICE

Don't let your ego or stubbornness keep you from getting advice that can get you on a much faster track to your fitness goals. I can't stress this enough. Too many people are literally spinning their wheels and getting nowhere. One wouldn't just try and go build a house without any knowledge or advice on how to do so, yet I see so many people blindly jump into a diet or exercise routine. Doing so just makes it that much harder than if they just sought out some help.

An absolute must with advice, is ensuring that it is from a credible source.

That is very tricky to find and to know in today's world, as there are numerous books, workout videos, podcasts and articles. I remember being quite confused about what to believe and trust when I started my health and fitness journey years ago, and at times still am.

For example, I read an article about the need to avoid carrots in your diet because of the believed impact it had on your sugar levels. I thought to myself, "This seems ridiculous, how can a nutritious, health promoting and low-calorie vegetable be something that we should avoid eating?" I decided to file it away and do more research on it. In my research, I still found plenty of articles stating to stay away from carrots, but I noticed that they weren't from credible sources. Then I found more in-depth, scientific and fact-based articles that stated that carrots were absolutely fine to eat, and that there was no reason not to include them in your diet. I then discredited the carrot fallacy and filed it under, "OK to eat carrots" in the fact section.

Don't always believe everything you see or hear.

Consider the source and file it away in your mind under "Needs More Information." There is a lot of conflicting information out there, so take everything with a grain of salt, whether it's something you read, something someone told you or what you heard on television.

When it comes to personal trainers, the same applies. Some have little experience or limited knowledge, and can actually be quite dangerous to work with. There are trainers that could be misinforming their clients or not correcting bad form. I've witnessed personal trainers on their cell phones while working with clients, and not paying any attention. I've even witnessed trainers watching a client do an exercise with poor form and not correct them. I was horrified. And this poor person was paying a lot of money for their time. Some trainers really know how to sell themselves, as they may be muscular and fit, and look the part. BUT It doesn't always mean that they truly provide sound, solid advice and are a good, quality trainer. This is a "don't always believe what you see" scenario.

My advice: look for trainers with experience and interview them. Make sure a trainer will start you out at the appropriate level that you need. I find some trainers greatly overwork clients that are true beginners, making them so sore that they can barely move for days. They overtrain them, fail to start them off at an appropriate level or progress them too fast. Be very careful with whom you select. I hate to see people seek help and advice, which is ideal to help you start on the right track, only to be overtrained and misled. This can discourage someone from working with a quality trainer that can help them get on track, stay on track and really help them achieve their goals.

There are some amazing trainers out there, and some very knowledgeable and trustworthy people providing sound, practical, inspiring and empowering help and advice. The best advice I can give you — have a thirst for knowledge and keep learning.

**Knowledge is power, and a crucial component
of a foundation's strength.**

The more you increase your knowledge, the more you increase the strength of your foundation. Put that knowledge into action to get on track and stay on track!

"If you focus on results, you will never change. If you focus on change, you will get results."
—*Joydeep Meena*

WEIGH NOT

Why is it that so many people are obsessed with weighing themselves? What will it take to keep people from constantly stepping on the scale and making comments and judgments about what the scale says versus understanding what's really going on with their body? Yes, there are some people that really do need to drop a few pounds, or maybe several pounds, but the number on the scale should NOT be the sole focus of all your efforts. Why not? Well, let me explain.

Scale weight

When you only focus on wanting to see the numbers on the scale drop, you're likely to get frustrated and give up on your workouts. When someone starts a new exercise routine, they typically gain muscle and lose fat (reduce body fat), but the scale only shows your total body weight. If you gain 2 lbs. of muscle and lose 2 lbs. of fat, the scale will remain unchanged.

Not seeing the scale budge can often leave people mistakenly frustrated and defeated.

They get discouraged and want to quit, when in actuality they're making positive and more beneficial changes in their body than they might realize. They could in actuality be losing body fat, and not know it, or just be experiencing normal fluctuations in their weight.

Weight Fluctuations

If you weigh yourself first thing in the morning, you're lighter. If you weigh yourself at night before you go to bed, you're heavier, and in the morning your lighter again. Does this mean you gained weight? Yes, but in a temporary sense. Think about it, you gain weight throughout the day by eating and drinking water. Food and water have weight, as they don't evaporate when you ingest them. That alone will cause your "scale" weight to go up, but it's just the weight of the food and water you consumed.

Just because you see the scale go up doesn't necessarily give you a reason to go screaming at the numbers you see between your feet.

For example, sodium can cause your body to retain more water (you gain weight). After exercise, you can have an immediate, temporary loss of water (you lose weight). This weight gain and loss is entirely water, just normal fluctuations that your body goes through throughout the day and on an ongoing basis.

Another thing to consider is muscle glycogen stores. Carbohydrates are stored in your muscles as glycogen. When carbs are stored as glycogen, they pull in 3–4 grams of water with each gram of carbs they store. I like to use the analogy of a dry sponge versus a wet sponge. A dry sponge is like a muscle depleted of its energy stores (glycogen); all the water is squeezed out making it lighter in weight.

When you eat carbohydrates and replenish your muscle glycogen, it's like a dry sponge filling up with water, which makes it heavier.

The carbs replenish the muscle glycogen in the muscle (dry sponge) and pull water in with it as it's stored. When your muscles replenish their energy stores, it's just like a sponge filling up with water. The wet sponge weighs more than the dry sponge. Make sense?

Body Fat Scales

Ideally, the best kind of scale to have is one that calculates body composition. This is by far much better than using a body weight scale, as the scale does not tell you anything about what compromises your weight. There are two main types, one is called a Body Fat Scale and the other a Full Body Composition Analyzer Scale. They both will function as an ordinary scale, but the difference with these body composition scales is that they can calculate your body composition — body fat percentage, lean body mass (muscle) and hydration levels. Some more advanced scales can calculate subcutaneous fat, visceral fat, bone mass and metabolic age. Honestly, I wouldn't trust the scales to provide accurate information with those more advanced options. In my opinion, those kinds of numbers should only be trusted from tests performed by medical professionals — for example, a bone density test.

How do these scales work? To analyze your body composition, you input some basic info like height and age — then you simply step on the scale with bare feet. The scales use bioelectric impedance technology (a small electric current that travels through your body) to analyze your body composition. After about five seconds, the scale will give you a reading with your body composition stats. The speed of which that current travels is what is used to make the body composition calculations. Muscle has more water than fat, so if someone has a high amount of muscle (and less body fat), the current will travel faster than someone with less muscle (and more body fat).

The Full Body Composition Analyzer has a bar you hold on to when you step on the scale. This is claimed to help it be a more accurate total body calculation. The stand-on scales' electrical current only travels through the lower half of the body, versus the upper and lower body with the Full Body Analyzer.

Using the body fat scales are far better than using a weight-only scale, but it's important to realize that they are not known to have a high level of accuracy.

Be aware though, if you're dehydrated it can make your body fat percentage read higher. I recommend using the scale on a weekly basis, to track body fat, lean body mass and hydration levels. You want to see your body fat percentage drop, your muscle mass maintained (or increase) and your hydration levels optimized. Although the accuracy of the body fat percentage itself may be inaccurate, it is still valuable to know, as it still can be used to show changes in body composition. For example, say I'm 20% body fat in reality, but the scale says I'm 30%. Even though that 30% number is much higher and not accurate, if that 30% drops to 28%, then 25%, it is still showing that I am losing body fat. A weight-only scale will not.

A body composition scale is the best way to go to truly measure your progress, but remember that the focus needs to be on losing body fat, not just scale weight.

In addition, we need to remind ourselves of all the health benefits exercise offers and focus on accomplishing those. Focus on being more active, having more energy, getting your heart more conditioned and adding years to your life. See the whole picture, not just the numbers on the scale.

There are other numbers, as in our health stats, that are vitally important to our overall health and well-being.

Why not focus on lowering your cholesterol, resting heart rate or blood pressure? Start giving those numbers the value they deserve and quit the obsession with the scale. By focusing on more meaningful goals, you are more likely to stick with your fitness routine, see results and not get frustrated. Guess what? In turn, you will drop the body fat and lose the weight after all.

"Deciding to commit yourself to long term results rather than short term fixes is as important as any decision you'll make in your lifetime."
—Anthony Robbins

SILLY SALLY — A TALE OF THE SCALE

The scale. What does that number between your feet really tell you? If you see the scale go up, you're gaining weight and something must be terribly wrong with your diet. If you see it going down, that's good, so you must be doing everything right. If this describes your belief about the scale, you can be terribly misled. Why? To explain, I'll tell you a little story about two ladies — Silly Sally and Buff Betty.

Silly Sally weighs herself every morning. On a Monday morning, Silly Sally gets on the scale and weighs 3 pounds more than she did Saturday morning. Silly Sally doesn't understand how she could have gained 3 pounds in just 2 days. She thinks to herself — I can't believe I gained 3 pounds, I'm getting fat! What Silly Sally doesn't know is that the extra scale weight was just water retention from eating foods high in sodium the day before.

Because of the 3-pound gain, Silly Sally starts working out and eating better, very determined to lose the 3 pounds she thinks she's gained. After a few weeks of workouts and eating healthier, she steps on the scale to see that it's a pound heavier than when she first started. Silly Sally can't believe she's gained weight from her healthy regimen. In fact, she's so upset she decides to just go back to her old ways of eating whatever she wants and not exercising. She weighed less then, so to her, that was obviously working.

Buff Betty rarely weighs herself, for she knows that weighing yourself doesn't give you a true measure of progress. Buff Betty started an exercise program several weeks ago and has started eating healthier as well. At the beginning of it, she got her body fat measured so she knew what her starting body composition was. Buff Betty's body composition test showed that she was at 30% body fat. Since she weighed 150 pounds, this meant that 30% of her weight was body fat (45 pounds).

Buff Betty knows that when trying to lose weight it's important to make sure you're only losing body fat, and not muscle (lean body mass). After a few weeks of working out, she notices her clothes fitting looser and she can see a difference in the mirror — her arms and legs are much more toned and defined. She steps on the scale out of curiosity, and it's up a pound. She's not frustrated at all, because she knows that she is losing body fat and doesn't care what she weighs. She can fit into her skinny jeans, so she thinks to herself, "Who cares what the scale says!"

Buff Betty gets her body composition re-checked after a few weeks. Buff Betty was right, for her body fat has dropped from 30% to 28%. Although she was 1 pound heavier on the scale, she was leaner and had less body fat then she did at 150 pounds. This is because she lost fat and gained muscle. In Buff Betty's case, she lost 2.7 pounds of fat and gained 3.7 pounds of muscle — resulting in a 1-pound increase on the scale. Buff Betty is elated and decides to treat herself to another pair of skinny jeans.

Weeks later, Silly Sally and Buff Betty happen to meet in a jean store at the mall. Silly Sally is buying "fat jeans" and Buff Betty is there to buy her "skinny jeans." Silly Sally sees Buff Betty picking out jeans and says, "I'm jealous of your great figure. I bet you only weigh about 125 pounds. I really wish I weighed that!"

Buff Betty replies, "Actually, I weigh a little over 150 pounds."

Silly Sally is quite impressed and exclaims, "Wow, you look so thin and toned; I would have never guessed that!"

"Well, I'm toned because I built muscle, and I am leaner because of it. And muscle weighs more than fat."

"How is that?"

"It's because a pound of muscle takes up much less space than a pound of fat. Technically a pound is a pound, but if you have a pound of each, the fat amount would be about double the size of the much more compact muscle."

"I get it now. I can't believe I've been so silly, what was I thinking? Can we workout together sometime?

"Sure, just promise me you won't be one of those girls that weighs herself all the time."

"OK, I think I've learned my lesson."

4

THE ROOF – MINDSET

MINDSET — IT REALLY MATTERS

Our mindset plays a critical role in coping with life and the ability to achieve success. One's mindset is just like the roof of a house. In good shape, it protects the interior of a home from the elements. In poor shape, it can leak and lead to damage of the internal structures (including the pillars and foundation).

In order for our bodies (aka the house we live in) to be protected, we need a strong and protective mindset.

A positive mindset is a like having a strong and sturdy roof.

It will protect us from the harsh elements of life — like stress and the struggles of life. On the other hand, a negative mindset, is like having a leaky roof.

Think about the following examples:

Leaky Roof -> Erodes Pillars (diet and exercise plan)

Example: negative thinking will affect your diet and exercise motivation

Roof Collapses -> Pillars Erode

Example: having a negative attitude will lead to reduced efforts, not eating as healthy or exercising as much

Pillars Erode -> Pillars Fall

Example: having a bad attitude and wanting to quit a healthy eating plan or exercise routine

No roof -> Cracks in Foundation

Example: a negative mindset can keep someone from experiencing happiness and properly taking care of themselves

Over time, the leaks will erode away and can cause damage to our pillars (diet and exercise plan) and our foundation.

The section will help teach you how to build a strong and sturdy roof. You will learn how to master your mind, increase your motivation, learn from your slip ups, be consistent, disciplined, and mentally strong. You got this!

"When you master your own mind, anything is possible."
—*Sanchit Yadav*

MASTER YOUR MIND, MASTER YOUR BODY

Maybe you've talked yourself out of going to the gym, or maybe you gave in to those cookies calling your name in the middle of the night. Or maybe you think there's no hope for you, that you're never going to be able to be able to be "fit" or lose the weight that you want to. Oftentimes, negative thinking will lead to lapses in our workout regimen or our diet.

Our thoughts control our actions, and if you don't see yourself achieving your fitness and weight loss goals, it's likely you'll get what you think.

If you can't see yourself being successful, and don't believe in yourself, you are more than likely going to fail. What's hard for people that are trying to lose weight, is that seeing is believing for them. It's something that you personally can't see because when you see yourself in the mirror, your mind views it "as is."

One of the hardest parts about getting started on an exercise or weight loss program is motivation, and then it's staying motivated once you start.

Once you start seeing results, that tends to motivate you, and then you're all gung-ho and ready to go. In between the starting part and the point where you finally start seeing results is where the battle occurs. That's what can seem like the steepest uphill climb you've ever experienced. That road can be short for some, but a longer, tougher road for others.

There are several factors that determine how fast someone will see results on an exercise and/or diet program — like diet history, current dietary and exercise practices, sleep schedule, stress, alcohol use and medications. Some people may have a longer, harder road than others because of poor dietary practices in the past. They may be starting off with a slower metabolism than others, so mastering their mind is going to be just as important as mastering their metabolism.

I believe knowledge brings understanding, and with understanding, hope.

When you have hope, you have motivation. You finally have a feeling of, "Yes, I can do it!" With all that knowledge, hope and motivation, guess what comes next? You got it, success!

With knowledge comes power, not only to master your mind but your body.

Believe it, believe in yourself, and you'll achieve the results you long for!

Mind Over Muffin Top Activity

Identify with the changes you want to make and be the change.

Write them down.

I am someone that _____

I am someone that _____

I am someone that _____

Example:

I am someone that <u>drinks water everyday</u>

I am someone that <u>takes evening walks</u>

I am someone that <u>is getting healthier</u>

"You must learn a new way to think before you can master a new way to be."
—Marianne Williamson

THE POWER OF POSITIVE THINKING

Maintaining a positive mindset and outlook on life, and having hope, can help you maintain high levels of motivation during stressful times. Try to focus on the good and keep working towards positive goals in your life. Pull yourself up, think positive thoughts, and be grateful for the positive things in your life.

Focusing on the good helps increase mental strength and resilience, allowing us to stay motivated and *keep an upper hand* on stress.

We must become a master of our thoughts to learn how to think differently and behave differently (change for the better). It boils down to this — we think, we feel, we do. If we think <u>negative</u> thoughts, we feel <u>negative</u> thoughts about ourselves, and we engage in <u>negative</u> behaviors – all stemming from that initial negative thought.

Example:

I think — "I won't be able to lose weight." (negative)

I feel — "I feel sad and unworthy because of my weight." (negative)

I do — "I tend to eat a lot of cookies and cakes because I'm upset." (negative)

On the flip side, if we think <u>positive</u> thoughts, we feel <u>positive</u> thoughts, and we engage in <u>positive</u> behaviors.

Example:

I think — "I'm going to try my best to lose weight." (positive)

I feel — "Proud of myself for taking steps to improve my health." (positive)

I do — "I eat fruit or a healthy alternative when I crave sweets." (positive)

Don't give life to negative thoughts by speaking them. It's one thing to think them, another to say them. Spoken words "take seed" in our minds. Keeping your mind positive takes keeping your spoken words positive, which allows the positive seeds to blossom in your mind.

Our thoughts drive our emotions, behavior and our physiology.

We can have overrigid patterns of thinking, errors in our logic and just bad mental habits in general. What one thinks in their mind can be distorted and inaccurate.

Our own thoughts can get in the way of productive emotions. Be aware of any limiting thoughts or beliefs you may have. There is always a way to reframe the way you see things.

Practice self-compassion with yourself — think and speak kindly. When we have judgments about ourselves, it can increase our stress levels, which in turn increases cortisol. Love yourself, you are worthy, and you are worthy of having a happier and healthier life.

Did you know?

Optimists live on average 15 years longer than pessimists

Mind Over Muffin Top Activity

When it comes to choosing our words, avoid using:

"I should _____"

"I need to _____"

"I have to _____"

These are more negative and it doesn't motivate us to want to do them.

Instead, if we change our thoughts to:

"I want to _____"

"I can _____"

Thinking in this way is more empowering, and we will be much more motivated to take action.

What are some common "I should", "I need to", or "I have to" statements you make?

How can you reword those statements using more empowering phrases like "I want to" and "I can"?

"Human beings, by changing the inner attitudes of their minds, can change the outer aspects of their lives."
—*William James*

BE YOUR OWN CHEERLEADER

Are you being your own best cheerleader? We are nice to our friends, support them and believe in them (or at least I hope so) — but with ourselves, we tend to be our own worst enemy. We beat ourselves up with negative self-talk and tell ourselves we can't do things. On the flip side, we could build ourselves up and think, "Yes, I can do this!"

This positive mindset and thinking in terms of "I can" creates action, and action creates change.

Maybe you want to start an exercise program, eat healthier or run in your first 5k. How many times have you told yourself you need to make some changes in your life? Thinking about doing it is not enough. Not only do we need to take action, but we need to envision and believe in what we want to achieve.

You have to believe it before you can achieve it.

If you don't believe you can do something, you are likely going to fail. A huge part of the achieving results equation is believing in yourself. Positive thoughts lead to positive actions. Negative thoughts lead to inaction. If you think negative thoughts, chances are you will speak of yourself in a negative way. Even if you are overweight and out of shape, don't get down on yourself. You can lose weight and you can get in shape.

Every in-shape person was once out of shape. What did they do? They didn't just think about it, they took action.

**Don't keep thinking about the changes you
want to make, start doing them.**

Your gym shoes aren't going to jump on your feet every morning and take you for a walk, nor is my oatmeal going to cook itself. Eliminate the "why you haven't started," and make a plan to make it easier for "why you can." Believe in yourself, and make it happen!

"Forget all the reasons why it won't work and believe the one reason why it will."
—Ziad K. Abdelnour

STOP THE "I CAN'T" BUS

When it comes to your health, are you actually doing what you know you should be doing? Are you making choices in your life to improve your health and the quality of your life — or are you just doing the opposite?

Doing

Most people who know better often have a long list of excuses for why they can't do what they know they should do. The problem arises when you allow your excuses and negative "I can't" thinking to take control of your life and your health.

You have the choice, you just need to be willing to start and to try.

Starting is the hardest part. If you get your gym shoes on, you will more than likely get yourself out the door — to walk, to the gym, etc. If you get yourself out the door, even better. Think in terms of what you can do versus what you can't. What are things you can do to start making positive changes in your health?

Action creates change, and doing something is better than doing nothing.

If you can think in terms of what you *can do*, you can make positive changes and improve your health and fitness levels.

Changes

What are things you can do?

You can make it a priority to get more sleep.

You can make it a priority to fit exercise in your schedule.

You can pack food and eat out less often.

You can make healthier food choices.

You can drink more water.

You can, you can, you can. You can make changes. Even as insignificant as some may seem, they can lead to tremendous positive changes in the quality of your life.

"It's not what we do once in a while that shapes our lives, it's what we do consistently."
—Tony Robbins

CONSISTENTLY CONSISTENT

Consistency, how often are you practicing it to achieve your goals? As with any goal you have, you need to achieve it when it comes to your health and fitness. If you're trying to lose weight, are you going to be able to achieve that by only eating healthy every once in a while? Are you going to be able to get in shape if you only work out a day *here and there?*

If you're consistent with an exercise routine and eating healthy, in time the weight will come off and your shape will improve.

Unfortunately, I find many of us struggle with being consistent. We don't see the results that we want and give up hope. It is estimated that 50% of new exercisers quit in the first six months. But you are not going to be one of those people.

Be patient. We are a society that values immediate rewards. We need to have the ability to have the patience to allow the rewards we're creating for our future to develop. And most importantly, we need to be consistent.

Being consistent with one's actions, and with one's choices, is what is needed and necessary to achieve the forward progress you need to achieve your goals.

Consistency leads to progress, progress leads to results, and results lead to success.

Appreciate the progress you get → Happiness → Continue going → Better results

So, what can you do to help you be more consistent with achieving your health and fitness goals?

Start implementing the 5 Ps!

1. **Plan** — Think ahead and plan. Make a list of foods you need so you have it on hand when you shop. Plan what and when you're going to eat every day. If you just *wing* what you're eating every day, you'll have no idea if you're eating properly. With workouts, schedule them like you would an appointment. Plan your meals and workouts into your day so it works with your schedule. If you fail to plan, you plan to fail.

2. **Purchase** — Eating healthy starts at the market. Having healthy food options for meals and snacks is key to diet success. Do not purchase foods that you know you tend to overeat or aren't healthy for you.

3. **Prepare** — It won't help you to have healthy foods at home if you don't use them and they go to waste. When you cook, make extra so you have leftovers to use so you don't have to cook as often. Make salads ahead of time and put into storage containers or glass jars with lids. The sooner you prepare foods after you purchase them the better, then you're less likely to forget and more likely to use them.

4. **Pack** — Bringing your own healthy meals and snacks, either to work or when you're on the go, saves money, calories and helps you have more "stick-to-it-ive-ness." You're more likely to stray and eat junk food, or eat out, if you don't have your own food on hand.

5. **Portions** — You *can* have too much of a good thing, as in eating too much of even a healthy food. For example, sweet potatoes are very nutritious and good for you, but eating too many isn't. Proper portion sizes with all foods are necessary to keep your calories *in check* and to eating a balanced diet.

"Make time for it. Just get it done. Nobody ever got strong or in shape by thinking about it. They did it."
—*Jim Wendler*

DISCIPLINE AND CHOICES

How many times have you heard someone say, "I'm going to start my diet Monday"? Maybe you even said it yourself recently. I can't even say I'm not guilty of saying it myself (secretly to myself of course). What I've realized is, that people tend to justify eating whatever they want with a future promise to work it off. One might say, "I can eat this cheeseburger and fries today, I'll run it off tomorrow" or "I can have this hot fudge sundae today, I'll work out tomorrow."

Oh yeah, really?

I bet at least 50% of the time we promise to work something off that it never happens. OR say you *do* workout that next day, more than likely you won't burn off as many calories as you took in.

The fact is that the weight goes on very easily, but it's not easy to get off.

Then there are the people that have a set date that they're starting a diet. They finally have made the decision that they need to lose some weight, yet go out and stuff themselves on junk food before they start it. It's like it's their *last supper*. They tell themselves they know that they can't have the junk food on their diet, so they're eating it now because they can't eat it later. Well, guess what? Now you probably have a few more of those stubborn pounds to get off AND it will be even harder to fight off those junk food cravings.

Eating high-fat and high-sugar foods, like ice cream and donuts for example, cause your body to crave sugar and fat. Now it will be even harder to avoid eating ice cream and donuts because you're going to crave them that much more. Well, you have to be able to live a little, right? Yes, but that's it precisely. You will be "living a little" — living a little less longer — the more you do decide to eat these junk foods. I'm sure we all would love to be able to eat whatever we want without the repercussions, but the fact is that foods high in sugar are just bad for us, and bad for our bodies.

There is always a healthier alternative, you just need the discipline and desire to make the smarter choice.

What do you want more? Do you really want to eat that donut, or would you much rather be able to fit into your jeans? I honestly dread doing cardio most days, but I tell myself I dislike not being able to fit into my jeans more than I dread the cardio. Strive to always keep your fitness and weight loss goals in mind, and make choices that will help you to achieve them.

Everything in life is a choice, and where you are right now is a result of all the choices you have made in the past.

No, you didn't have to eat pie for dinner last night because you were too busy to eat anything else, you chose to. Hopefully now you won't think like that anymore, and you will make the CHOICE to be a healthier, fitter you.

Discipline = Self Love (not punishment)

You can choose your actions but can't choose the consequences.

"You can't go back and make a new start, but you can start right now and make a brand new ending."
—James R. Sherman

LAPSE AND LEARN

Have you noticed all the derailments around town lately? The broken wagons? If you haven't caught on yet, I am not talking about trains or wagons. I am referring to all the people that *fell off the wagon"* — have fallen off track with their fitness goals.

Do you think a boxer goes into a ring thinking he'll never get knocked down? If a boxer gets knocked down, doesn't try to get back up and just gives up, how is that boxer ever going to win a battle? Rocky wouldn't be much of a fighter if he didn't get back up every time he got knocked down.

When it comes to any kind of battle, whether in a boxing ring or fighting the war against fat, giving up just isn't part of a winning strategy. Winning takes perseverance, and it takes determination. Just because you slip up and give in to that donut at work, doesn't mean you sabotaged your entire plan.

Lapses like this are bound to happen, but the key is to realize that a lapse is a single event.

Look at it as a way to learn, as in why it happened and why you chose to eat it. Maybe you skipped breakfast that day, or you allowed negative self-talk to take over. If you slip up, take control, and get back on track.

189

You don't want to turn a little slip up of eating one donut into eating a whole box. Learn from your mistakes (lapses) and you can help lessen the chances you will give in to that donut again. Eat breakfast and pack a cooler of healthy foods and snacks to have on hand, and you will find it much easier to resist that donut.

Of course, striving for 100% compliance with a fitness and nutrition program is ideal, but not likely to happen. Don't you think you will get better results sticking to something 80–90% of the time versus following it 50% of the time? Even if you improve 50%, then increase it gradually, that is better than not making any changes at all. Focus on making progress, not perfection. It does not take perfection to make progress.

Failures are learning opportunities and are only failures if you do not keep moving forward and get back on track.

You only fail when you quit. Expect setbacks. There is no quick fix, and we can't skip the learning process. Just keep moving forward with steps, in taking action and doing what you can to make positive changes and stay on track with your goals.

If you *fall off the wagon*, get back on. If you veer off track a little, get back on. If you keep those wheels moving, you are getting somewhere, and that somewhere is success.

Did you know?

People tend to make more unhealthy choices in loud restaurants than places with soft music.

Mind Over Muffin Top Activity

On a weekly basis, think about what you accomplished and if you had any challenges. Ask yourself:

What went well?

What can I improve on?

Give yourself credit for what went well, not just what didn't. For what didn't go well, you can learn from it and put strategies in place to help your upcoming weeks be better. I refer to them as S.O.S. — Strategies for Ongoing Success! So, if you have a bad week, just put your S.O.S. into action!

"Mindfulness isn't difficult. We just need to remember to do it."
—Sharon Saltzberg

MINDFULNESS

When it comes to successful weight loss (losing weight and keeping it off), exercise and calorie counting typically come to mind for people. But what about the mind itself, as in mindful eating? New research is showing that mindfulness, when applied to eating, can assist with weight loss.

Tired of counting calories? Forgetting to log your food intake?

Maybe a little mindfulness is all you need.

I think we've all been guilty of mindless, or distracted eating. One example of this is going to the movies and eating popcorn. While watching a movie, you grab handful after handful of popcorn, and before you know it, you're scraping bottom. You ate far more than you intended to. Think of how often you find yourself sitting on the couch, watching television and eating more then you intended.

Research has shown that distracted eating increases the amount eaten by 10%.

Not only does mindless eating increase calorie consumption at a sitting, but it's also been shown to increase the total amount eaten later in the day by 25%. I think this warrants some caution tape being placed around your couch. In case you don't like my caution tape idea, here are some other suggestions to help.

Slow down

It takes about twenty minutes before your brain registers that you're full, so slow down when you eat. Take small bites and chew your food thoroughly;

this will take more time and also allow for optimal digestion. It's also believed that being distracted while you eat, for example driving or working, may affect your digestion. Our bodies' digestion can slow or stop from distractions or stress, similar to a "fight or flight" reaction. This decreases our bodies' ability to absorb nutrients from the food we eat.

Think Back

What and how much did you eat at your previous meal? Studies have shown that recalling food consumed at the previous meal decreased amount eaten by 10% at the following meal. Being conscious of your food intake throughout the day helps to keep your goals in mind and prevent careless eating.

Check Yourself

Before you open that refrigerator door, or get into the pantry searching for food, ask yourself if you are truly hungry — or just bored. If you choose to eat, then measure out a controlled amount of food and stick to it. Even if you've decided you're going to have milk and cookies, put a small amount on a plate and stick to eating that amount versus taking the whole bag to the couch.

Eliminate Trigger Foods

If one cookie leads to ten cookies, then that's a trigger food and you need to get it out, and keep it out of your home. Whether it's cookies, chips, ice cream or candy — whatever it is, if you can't control the amount you eat, it's not worth having around. Don't kid yourself when you tell yourself you can have it around, when you know deep down, you can't.

Limit Couch Time

If you're on the couch, you're not moving, and the likelihood of eating out of boredom increases. Try reading, doing puzzles or going for a walk. You may be too tired after work to go on a long or fast-paced walk, but a short leisurely stroll beats sitting on the couch eating a bowl of ice cream.

Mirrored Eating

Studies have found that women tend to mirror other women's eating habits. If you see someone bringing a cookie back to their desk at work, you're more likely to grab one yourself than if you didn't see it. Be the one to set a good example and not follow a bad one. Healthy habits can be just as contagious and are more rewarding in the long run.

Smell of See Food

The "out of sight, out of mind" idea works the best. If you have to look at a candy jar all day at work, there's going to be a time where you're likely to give in. If you smell cookies baking in the oven, you're going to want to eat one as soon as they come out of the oven. Leave the room, put on blindfolds and pinch your nose shut. I'm seriously just kidding, and realistically that's not going to work if you're at work. Try to be disciplined and avoid temptation. Keep your goals in mind, and remember it's a choice you make. Make healthier choices — your reward will be a healthier and happier body and mind.

Dehydrated

Try this skin pinch test: pinch the skin on the back of your hand. If it's slow in returning and doesn't spring right back, you're dehydrated. Some common signs of dehydration are sleepiness, low energy and believe it or not — hunger. If you feel thirsty you are already dehydrated.

"Life is not merely being alive, but being well."
—*Marcus Valerius Martialis*

DEFEATING DEPRESSION

Depression, whether you're just down in the dumps or have severe depression, is a condition that isn't much of a joy to experience. It can be debilitating and leave one feeling helpless and hopeless. But there are some things you can do to help, to at the least leave you feeling a little better, or hopefully a lot.

Exercise

Did you know that regular exercise can improve mood in people with mild to moderate depression, and may also play a role in treating severe depression?

Exercise can be a great alternative for those who wish to avoid the need for antidepressants.

One study showed that walking 35 minutes, 5 times a week, or 60 minutes, 3 times a week had a significant effect on mild to moderate depression symptoms. The effects of exercise actually lasted longer than antidepressants alone. The study also found that regular exercisers were less likely to relapse into depression.

Another study involved using three groups of participants — one group did aerobic exercise, another group took antidepressant meds and the third group did both: they exercised and took antidepressant meds.

Depression improved in all three groups, and 60–70% of the participants could no longer be classified as having major depression.

Research has also shown that exercise is an effective but underused treatment for mild to moderate depression.

Any form of exercise, be it walking, bike riding, swimming, or tennis, will offer some much-needed relief to sufferers of depression symptoms. Social support is also very important for those with depression, so group exercise, or exercising with a friend will offer even more benefits.

Even if you're not depressed, you'll find that exercise will help improve your mood and increase self-esteem. What have you got to lose? You can only feel better and it will improve your health.

Vitamin D

Reduced sun exposure can lead to depression, as the sun helps your body produce vitamin D. Less sun means less vitamin D. The lower one's levels of vitamin D, the higher the odds of experiencing depression. Have your levels checked by your health care provider to discuss using a supplement to increase your levels if needed.

Not able to get out in the sun much? Consider using a light box. Light box therapy is believed to help increase brain chemicals related to mood and depression — using just 30 minutes a day can help counter depression.

Sleep

Over 80% of people treated for depression experience symptoms of insomnia and have difficulty sleeping. Several studies have shown that people that suffer from insomnia are twice as likely to suffer from depression in the future, compared to those who don't have sleeping problems. Poor sleep has been found to negatively affect gut health, and poor gut health has been found to negatively affect sleep.

The better you eat, the better you can sleep, and the better you can feel. So, go take a hike, soak up some sun and get on the road to feeling better!

Mind Over Muffin Top Activity

Start rating how you feel before and after you exercise. On a scale of 1–10, rate your level of depression/happiness and your level of motivation. 1 will be feeling the lowest amount, and 10 will be the highest, and feeling the best.

For example, I had a day where I felt super tired, worn out and wasn't feeling much motivation at all. It was a day where I didn't get much sleep the night before, and I had a heck of a time talking myself into doing some sort of exercise.

Here's how I rated myself:

Depression/happiness = 5 out of 10 pre-exercise

7 out of 10 post-exercise

Motivation = 3 out of 10 pre-exercise

7 out of 10 post-exercise

As tired and unmotivated as I was, I felt an immediate sense of refreshment after I started moving. I still felt some fatigue in general, but at least I had a little more energy and motivation to make myself dinner and be a little productive.

Most people notice improvements, some more so than others. You can only feel better, and I guarantee you will never feel worse.

People suffering from severe mental illnesses, including depression and bipolar disorder, have a shorter lifespan. Some studies show a reduced life expectancy of as much as 15–30 years. Don't be afraid to ask for help if you need it. You are worthy and deserve to live a life of health and happiness.

"There are plenty of difficult obstacles in your path. Don't allow yourself to become one of them."
—Ralph Marston

MENTAL PROWESS

Resilience

Life is always going to present challenges. You have the ability to overcome, to get through the obstacle course of life and to keep moving in the direction of your goals. When you are confronted with obstacles, deal with them one at a time. Do not let obstacles deter you from achieving your dreams.

The strength and knowledge you gain from overcoming your obstacles will make it that much easier for you to get through future obstacles you encounter.

The more challenging the obstacle is in overcoming, the more rewarding it will be to have overcome it. Don't just try until it gets too hard and then give up.

Struggles are what change us for the better, and enable us to become stronger. As one of my clients brilliantly stated during a workout, "The struggle makes you stronger!"

Willpower

Don't make decisions based on emotions. Focus on the good habits you've created and do what you told yourself you're going to do. Relying on emotions and feelings to dictate our behaviors leads to failure. Relying on habits and rituals lead to success.

**Think you "will" have the "power" to
do this, and you will succeed.**

*"It's not what you say out of your mouth that determines your
life, it's what you whisper to yourself that has the most power!"*
—*Robert T. Kiyosaki*

STAYING STRONG

There's been a recall on cookies; they're making people's pants shrink.
I'm joking about the recall on cookies, but increased consumption is
leading people to feel like their pants have shrunk. Why? We're being
pressured into eating too many, both directly and indirectly.

Have you ever thought of how societal pressure has affected your diet?
I'm sure most of us couldn't be left alone in a room with a box of cookies
and not want to eat one, or two, or the whole box. Since you're reading
this article, let's assume (I'm hoping) you wouldn't eat the whole box.
For the sake of example, let's say a friend of yours was in that room with
you, and they started eating the box of cookies. Odds are you would start
eating a few cookies with him or her just because they were eating them.

**The odds of you overindulging would be even higher if
he or she suggested you share the cookies with them.**

"What's a couple of cookies?" one might ask you, to pressure you into
eating them. Granted it's more likely that you would have been able to
resist the temptation if you were alone, but a mere suggestion will likely
lead to you guiltily wiping crumbs off of your face before you know it.

**Studies have shown that people eat more when with others versus
eating alone.**

Social norms also influence food choices and amount eaten. If a participant was told another was making a high-calorie or low-calorie choice, it increased the likelihood that they would tend to follow suit. It was also similar with the amount of food eaten, whether the person went back for seconds or pushed their plate away.

Direct pressure also influences social eating.

A parent would likely be upset to find out that their kid was being bullied at school. Some parents may in fact be bullying others themselves, and not even realize it. They are bullying their co-workers, family and friends by pushing them to eat unhealthy foods. I make this comparison not to downgrade the severity of bullying in schools, but to make people aware of their unwanted and potentially harmful behavior. "Oh, a piece of cake isn't going to kill you," someone might say. There's nothing wrong with offering a piece of cake to someone, but it's the pressure to eat it if someone really doesn't want it. My intent is to make people aware of the implications of their "kind pressure" on others to eat something.

An innocent piece of cake for one, could turn into a dieting disaster for others.

One turns into two, then three pieces and so on — and the habit that was so hard to break, the weight that was so hard to lose, is gained back and then some. I've had several clients that struggle with the ability to say no to others. If they were offered a piece of cake, they would often eat it due to the pure fear of offending or angering the person offering it to them.

Unfortunately, if you're one that wants to eat healthy or stick to a diet plan, you're going to have to deal with diet sabotagers sooner or later.

What do you do when someone tries to pressure you into eating something you don't want? What if you just don't want that piece of cake? You can say, "No, thank you but I don't want any," or turn the tables and say, "Why don't' you have another piece of cake?"

Giving in and saying yes to a piece of cake when you don't want it is likely due to a need for approval. It's important to realize that this may have been a behavior of yours that contributed to your weight gain in the first place.

Focus on self-improvement versus seeking approval from others.

Agreeing to something to make someone else happy, and giving in, means you're not keeping an agreement with yourself. We don't hurt others, we hurt ourselves.

It also helps to realize that diet sabotagers may be acting out of quilt, anger, shame or envy — they too may have a hard time saying no. Be strong — you can say no, and say yes to yourself!

"I'm grateful for my struggle because without it, I wouldn't
have stumbled upon my strength."
—Alexandra Elle

THE GREATNESS OF GRATITUDE

Acknowledge the goodness in your life. Gratitude is associated
with happiness. It helps people feel more positive emotions,
deal with adversity and even improve their health.

Gratitude is something you can express in many ways:

Past — appreciating something or someone from your past, or thankful
for an element of your past

Present — appreciating what you have, not taking anything for granted

Future — having a positive, optimistic and hopeful attitude for your
future

In a University of Miami study, participants were divided into three
groups and asked to write a few sentences each week. One group wrote
about what they were grateful for during that current week (positive
emphasis). Another group wrote about events that upset or irritated them
(negative emphasis). And the third group wrote about events that affected
them, without an emphasis on being positive or negative (neutral).

At the end of the 10-week study, the group that wrote about what they were grateful for (positive emphasis) were found to have a more positive outlook and feel better about their lives.

In addition, they also found that this group exercised more and had less visits to their doctor versus the negative-emphasis group. What a wonderful bonus, and another thing to be grateful for!

Get in the habit of practicing gratitude on a daily basis.

In her book, "8 to Great," MK Mueller advises us to think of three things we are grateful for from the previous day (24 hours). She states that the key is to think of three NEW things every day, and not repeat them. For best results, she advises to share them with someone, either verbally or written, for one month.

It's amazing how having an attitude of gratitude can change how you feel, and even what you attract. Positive attracts positive, negative attracts negative. Life can be very challenging, with devastation, heartbreak and loss. No matter the circumstance, try to find something to be grateful for. It will bring hope and a glimmer of light in what can seem like never-ending darkness. You can only find a silver lining if you look for it.

"The road to success is always under construction."
—Lily Tomlin

THE ROAD TO SUCCESS

How do you envision your road to success? Is it a highway, a winding country road or like a steep, continual climb up a mountain? As much as we would like a high-speed highway to success, it's likely going to be a combination of all three.

There will be times when we make fast progress, like being on a highway. Then there will be times when we veer side to side, like a winding road, like when we get off track and struggle to gain that forward momentum. AND there will be times when we feel we're going up a steep mountainside, struggling to climb and make progress.

Along our journey, we're going to experience breakdowns and go through construction zones.

Things can temporarily delay the journey, but you can fix what's broken, find alternate routes if necessary, and get right back on the road and journey ahead. What is at the end of your road to success? You, and your new house of happiness and health.

With this book, I hope you have learned how you can not only conquer your muffin top, BUT that you can conquer your goals and have life-long health, happiness and success!

Not another diet book — *Mind Over Muffin Top* is an empowering guide that inspires and motivates us to change.

Want to achieve your fitness goals once and for all? Learn why it all starts with creating a solid foundation — managing stress, sleep, self-care, healthy habits, planning, time management, prioritizing self, life balance and creating a positive home environment. No matter what diet or exercise plan you follow, if you don't start out by developing a solid foundation, you're likely to fail.

It's not about finding the perfect diet or the perfect exercise plan — it's about making simple, sustainable changes. Strengthen your mind with key knowledge, develop the much-needed foundation needed for lasting change and create a mindset to believe and achieve.

Learn crucial diet and exercise knowledge to optimize results, and how to maintain a positive mindset to keep you on track and achieve your goals. This book will give you the tools you need to conquer your muffin top, conquer your goals and finally get results. Achieve your goals, and transform your life!

ABOUT THE AUTHOR

Cheryl started her fitness career in her hometown of Cincinnati, Ohio, where she lived the majority of her life. Her fitness journey started on stage, as a natural competitive bodybuilder, then transitioned into her work as a personal trainer. During a two-year stay in Columbus, she started teaching bootcamp classes and fell in love with the group atmosphere. This led to starting her own business, Got2workout, in which she offered one-on-one sessions, small group training and bootcamp classes.

Cheryl's journey later landed her in Port Huron, Michigan. Her passion to help others with their weight loss struggles inspired her to become both a certified weight management consultant and a certified fitness and nutrition specialist.

She established herself in the Port Huron fitness community through personal training in local gyms and teaching bootcamp classes in a rec center. Then *opportunity knocked*, and Cheryl answered. She took a leap of faith and opened up her own women's only fitness studio, Buff Bodies Bootcamp. Throughout her years in the fitness industry, Cheryl had taken note of the many women she encountered, some as clients, and others she had simply crossed paths with. She came to realize that a huge percentage of these women feared going to and working out at a gym. This inspired Cheryl to open a women's only studio that would create a welcoming, non-intimidating and supportive environment for women. BUT she also wanted to make it fun, for she believed if you have fun doing it, you'll look forward to it and keep coming back. Not wanting to leave the guys out, she eventually offered some co-ed classes and even worked with a local boy's hockey team.

Her "Have Fun Getting Fit" motto helped inspire and empower women of all ages to achieve their health and fitness goals. She taught there for eight years, during which time she started writing for the local paper, the *Times Herald*. Cheryl's "Matter of Fat" column featured articles on health, nutrition, exercise, self-help and motivation. Cheryl provided information in a simple, informative and light-hearted manner — inspiring and motivating people to take action for their health.

Currently, Cheryl lives in Clinton Township, Michigan, and works full time for a public mental health agency as a health mentor. She utilizes a recovery-focused philosophy to teach and empower clients to be healthier in body and mind through the incorporation of a healthy lifestyle.

Made in the USA
Monee, IL
28 June 2021

71869350R00125